Gold
Man
Review

Gold Man Review is published once a year by Gold Man Publishing in Salem, Oregon.

Subscriptions available at www.goldmanpublishing.com

The editors invite submissions of previously unpublished works of fiction, nonfiction, poetry, art, and photography. Manuscripts, photographs, and art work can be submitted at www.goldmanpublishing.com

Copyright 2012/2013 Gold Man Publishing / Gold Man Review LLC.
PO Box 8202, Salem, OR 97303
Printed by Gold Man Publishing
ISSN: 2162-8238
ISBN: 978-0-615-54935-4

Contents

It's Beautiful Out Here: *Matt Young*   1

Question for My Birth Mother: *Colette Tennant*   9

Deal Broken: *Erick Mertz*   10

Work (Copland in the Woods): *John Byrne*   17

If We Took a Deep Breath: *Patty Somlo*   18

Close the Door: *Mary Arana*   22

Rhosymedre: *Amy Miller*   24

Risk Management: *Marc Janssen*   25

An Interview with Mike Chasar   27

Campaign Song: *Mrs. A.J. Duniway*   37

Reasons: *Mrs. Ajax*   39

""'Siah's Vote": *Anonymous*   42

Wife Versus Horse: *[Author unknown]*   45

Katie Lee and Willie Grey: *Margaret Verne*   47

My Ship: *Florence Percy (pseudonym of Elizabeth Akers Allen)*   49

The Perplexed Housekeeper: *Mrs. F. D. Gage*   51

Cold Turkey Substitute (and Stuffing): *Thomas Farringer-Logan*   55

Angels of the Drunk: *Tim Pfau*   67

Me and the Trees: *Allyson Myers*   68

Peaches: *Lois Rosen*   69

BSM30: *Brandon McMullen*   71

Those Who Can't: *David Jordan*   72

A Gift Rejected: *Michal Ann McArthur*   82

Astroturf is Forever: *Matt Young*   95

Transmogrify: *Nyla Alisia*   101

A Well Matched Man: *Chelsea Bieker*   102

Criticism: *Rick Stoddart*   116

A Permanent Marker: *Rick Stoddart*   117

If I Wore Sensible Shoes: *Ginger Dehlinger*   118

Egret on the Willamette: *John Byrne*   119

No Curtain. No Scenery: *Sarah Angleton*   121

Mary Lou's Make-Over: *Mike Ritchey*   130

A Matter of Life and Death, Seemingly: *Patrick Hannon*   142

Late August Night: *Caitlin Diehl*   151

Silence and Me: *Dan Encarnacion*   152

Aposiopesis: *Dan Encarnacion*   153

Fidelity: *Rick Stoddart*   154

A Table in Space: *Amy Miller*   155

Fence: *Dan Encarnacion*   157

Through the Window: *Grahame Watt*   159

I Heard You Were Dead: *Tim Pfau*   165

The Demise of J.N. Rainey: *Michael Snider*   166

A Time for Mourning: *Robert Bennett*   177

Rousseau's War: *Colette Tennant*   187

Meet the Contributors   188

Letters from the Editors

In this issue of Gold Man Review we wanted to celebrate the pioneer spirits of the men and women of yesteryear and today who dared the unknown road.

But what exactly embodies a pioneer? A pioneer does not buckle under hardship when they encounter obstacles in their path. A pioneer does not stray when others have turned from the trail. A pioneer never says "I can't" when the passage seems impossible. A pioneer is a dreamer, an innovator, and a groundbreaker. A pioneer holds on when all others have said to let go and keeps one foot before the other when everyone else has stopped. Just like the writer, the pioneer sees possibilities beyond the next bend where new worlds wait to be discovered.

That spirit of being a pioneer spurred us on this year, hovering in the periphery as we looked for pieces of writing that had something pioneering about it, in terms of originality as well as in terms of strength, determination, resilience, or understanding. With Gold Man himself as our mascot, our icon, our totem, the pioneer spirit couldn't help but rub off on us at Gold Man Review and teach us a thing or two. We learned so much this last year, but the most important thing we learned is that the pioneer spirit is alive in all of us.

And to all the pioneers who helped make Gold Man Review Issue 2, we thank you.

Onward,

Editor-in-Chief
Heather Cuthbertson

Project Editor
Nicklas Roetto

Managing Editor
Richard Beckham

Executive Editor
Marilyn Ebbs

Senior Editor
Darren Howard

Special Thanks to:
Samuel Hall
Rachel Lofton
Mary-Gray Mahoney
Sandra McDow

10 Must Haves
on the
Oregon Trail

It's Beautiful Out Here
Matt Young

Winter in the desert. Outside, roof runoff splashes the smell of plywood into the piss-soaked mud. Inside, the floor is littered with the bodies of sleeping marines separated by olive drab sleeping pads twenty inches wide. I own those twenty inches. Inside those twenty inches, I am the warm glowing happy center of the world.

Beyond the high concrete walls and razor wire surrounding our compound, through the rain, barking dogs, and sporadic gunfire, I hear the call to prayer. Five times a day, without fail the Shi'i Imams call the people of Fallujah to profess, "There is no god but God and Muhammad is His prophet."

I'm in my skivvies, cross-legged, staring at nude pictures of a woman whom I'll never meet, let alone touch. I haven't gotten an erection in two weeks. I wonder what she would look like if a .50 caliber BMG ball round tore through her thoracic cavity.

I haven't slept since we've been on rest and refit. Three days, seventy-two hours, four thousand three hundred and twenty minutes—I'm still calculating the seconds. I want to sleep. I want to sleep more than I want to get a hard-on. Every time I lay down, the desert chokes me, the stink of it, the feel of it. I can taste it on my tongue. I shake my fist and threaten violence, but I'm never satisfied.

I think I could sleep if I were home. If I were home in Indiana it would be all right. There would be snow instead of rain, warm beds, soft bodies, and toilets. But that isn't true. I have a brother there. He works for a technology company, something-or-other ending in "yne." He married last year to a woman who recently gave birth to his first child, a daughter named Emily. I've never met either of them. When I write him, he answers in vague clichés like, "Marty, there are good days and bad days."

I want to tell him that, here, there are only bad days.

My mother, after divorcing my drunk of a father, jumped on the born-again Christian train with her new Methodist revival preacher husband, and never looked back. I write her every once in a while, but all the responses tell me to "Look to God" or, "His divine providence will light the way." Mr. Martin, my father, hasn't been seen since the divorce six years ago. I like to think he's dead.

"I need to get out of here," I say.

"No one's stopping you, Marty," says Flynn, to my right. He calls me Marty because I told him I hate my last name. This way, he thinks, it's different. He's lying on his sleeping bag, spitting tobacco into an empty water bottle, and reading a letter from his wife, who lives in Inola, Oklahoma. I want to ask him to let me read the letter. It would be nice to see the scrawling feminine handwriting, smell the faint remnants of whatever fragrant soap she uses on her skin. Skin that isn't covered in dirt, blood, and bruises. I could sleep next to skin like that.

I actually feel good about home when Flynn talks about it. We went out one night before we left, about four months ago. He bought beers. I drank most of them. We were on the beach outside of base, and I walked to the end of the pier. An old legless Vietnam veteran wearing dirty olive drab fatigues sat at the pier lookout. His rusty wheelchair creaked as he played folk songs on a beat-up guitar. I remember looking at the stumps of his legs and crying, saying that I didn't want to die. The vet kept strumming the guitar, singing softly. Flynn only put his arm around my shoulders, led me away, and talked about home until I stopped; then we went back to base. I tell him often that I'm going to move to Oklahoma.

"I can't get it up," I say. He looks at me and shrugs. He's a muscular farm boy with a deep permanent tan and sleepy eyes. His hair is salt and pepper before his time. Combined with his dirty face, it makes him seem wise.

"Rain stopped, wanna burn one?" he asks. I tell him I do. His drawl calms me down. I let him do most of the talking so I can hear his voice. He tells me about his wife. I like hearing about her. He talks about how they've known each other all their lives and they were neighbors and high school sweethearts. He tells me about Inola and how small it is, only a class of twenty-three.

I imagine one day showing up on the small front porch of Flynn's house. His wife answers the door. She wears a yellow cotton sundress that billows around her knees, wisps of her blond hair blow across her face. I think that her hair must be blonde. I can't picture her any other way. She puts her arms around me and hugs me close as I cry into her milky neck. She tells me that it was a nightmare. That I don't have to worry. That I'm safe.

Flynn hooks the wedge of tobacco from his lip and drops it into the water bottle. He nudges me and motions with his chin toward the door.

I dress. The nubuck of my boots is salted and cracking from the fields we've been slogging through the past three months. I bend and twist them, checking for holes.

I scan the dim, creaking longhouse for Flynn, who stands by the door, having already navigated the maze of bodies and cots. I follow what I assume is his same path. Over mountains of men, packs, sleeping bags, camouflage utilities, and guns, I make my way.

The tip of my boot catches the softness of a body. Sterile tubing snakes from the emaciated arm that belongs to my radio operator, Wilson. The intravenous bag connected to the tubing drips rapidly to replace the fluids his body is losing to dysentery. A clear brownish puddle forms at the cuff of Wilson's trousers. His eyes remain shut. I envy him.

The air outside is frigid. The moisture hangs heavily around my fleeced shoulders. The suction of the mud pulls on the square of rotted plywood Flynn and I shift our feet upon. I can see the ghost outlines of four white PVC piss tubes jammed into the ground about fifty meters from where we stand. The earth around them is swollen and flooded, leaking the stinking underworld to the surface and into my nostrils. Between exhales of thick, acrid foreign cigarette smoke, my breath puffs in front of my face.

I would kill for a Camel or a Marlboro, but instead I'm smoking Pines. They are harsh and dry. I traded an Iraqi kid in exchange for some candy on our last patrol a few days ago. They are all I have.

"It's nice tonight," Flynn says. I inhale the rain and urine and mud and plywood and shit.

"You're fucked, Flynn."

"How do you figure?" His face turns to meet mine, awash in the insipid moonlight.

"The desert is shit. Everything in it is shit. Me, you, everything outside the wire. Hell, Wilson's inside basically bleeding shit," I say. We could be having a conversation over dinner or during the seventh inning stretch at a baseball game. I wish all this was the past. I dream we are outside on a warm Oklahoma day. His wife serves us iced tea, and we talk about worse times that make us feel alive and appreciative.

"You're just tired, Marty. We're all tired. It's nice tonight, I mean think about it. It stopped raining, we're on rest and refit," he pauses, "plus, no one's been hit in days." Another pause. "It's nice."

I close my eyes, breathing deep. The chill in the air numbs my nose against the smell of piss and burning human feces. The crackle of dry smoldering tobacco and the lazy roll of the Euphrates in the distance beat my eardrums. The lids of my eyes flutter open and I could be on the moon, it's so damn big. The door bounces against the water-bloated jam. I am not in Oklahoma, outside on a lawn drinking iced tea with Flynn and his wife. I am alone with the desert.

Another night and still I don't sleep. I lie in my bag and think about home. How bad do I want out of this shithole? A kid in another platoon shot himself in the foot so he could get out. The desert beat him. He lost faith in home and could not keep going. The thought of the small caliber bullet tearing through my boot, skin, tendon, muscle, and bone makes me gag. I decide I won't let it beat me.

I think about Flynn and the letter from his wife. He's always reading that letter. I've seen him read it during patrol breaks. He keeps it wrapped in a plastic sandwich bag in the breast pocket of his blouse, or in his flak jacket during missions. It's in his pocket now, about ten inches away from me.

I listen to the sounds of Flynn's sleep.

How nice it would be to read that letter. To feel like someone back home wanted me. My hand reaches out and hovers over the pocket with the name tape that reads, "U.S. Marines." I can almost smell her hair and feel her sun warmed skin wrapped around me. My fingertips caress the rough sweat stiffened fabric of his blouse. I can feel the outline of the tightly folded paper. So close.

Flynn rolls over and I retract my hand like a recoiling snake. I lie on my side and stare at it until morning.

A few days later, while on patrol outside of Fallujah we take a house as an observation post. A group of us stand around our interpreter as he instructs a woman where she can go to collect the money the United States Government will pay her as compensation for commandeering her house.

"Where will she stay?" I say to our interpreter.

"She has a brother she will stay with," he says. We watch the woman gather her five children and small flock of sheep and herd them down the mud road. The rest of the section takes gear from the trucks into the woman's house.

"Where's her husband? I didn't think women could own land," says someone from the back of the group.

"Her husband was killed by Americans last year. Probably for planting bombs in the road. Fucking terrorist, man," says the interpreter. He expatriated from Iraq in April of 1991 after collaborating with the United States military during Desert Storm. He holds full citizenship in the States. He's named Farroush, but tells everyone to call him Rambo.

One of the younger children, maybe five or six, breaks away from his mother and runs back toward us. Some of the guys give him candy or bread from their MREs. The boy moves to stand in front of Farroush. Farroush cuffs him on the cheek and says something in Arabic. There is a small exchange, and the boy runs away.

"What was that all about?" I ask.

"The boy, he has no strength, no faith, that is the problem with the younger generation. He said he must beg for food or he will starve. I tell him insha'Allah."

"What does it mean?"

"It means that, if God wills it, he will have food." Farroush walks away.

I watch the boy with no faith in his home, run to catch his family. I turn and take my gear into his house.

The widow's compound is a two-story concrete and stucco structure surrounded by a brick wall about six feet high. The windows have iron bars and no glass. The inside is cold, but clean and dry. All the rooms on the lower floor connect to one another.

I find Flynn in a large common room where everyone is setting up their sleeping bags and gear. He's sitting on his pack, once more reading the letter. He looks up and I feel my face redden. I want the letter. I think that he doesn't deserve to read the writing, that he's not good enough for her. If he was, he would write her every day. I've been writing letters to her in a notebook I keep in my pack.

I write about her soft skin and blonde hair. I write about long nights outside, watching the sun set and the stars come out. I write about small towns where everyone says hello to everyone else. I write that I need her. I write that I love her.

I imagine sending these letters. She responds that she loves me too, but she can't leave her husband. We live in silent desperation, she not wanting to destroy her faithful husband, and me not wanting to ruin our blood-forged friendship.

"Saved a spot for you," he says pointing at his side to the bare concrete.

"Thanks." My eyes don't meet his, but stay on the back side of the paper. Just a glimpse I think, just a millisecond of a glance at that writing. He folds it, replaces it, and removes a tin of chewing tobacco from his pocket and begins to pack his lip.

Twenty minutes later, we're on the roof, pulling guard duty, staring over barren mud fields in the fading foreign dusk. The sunset is a fiery ship sinking into the sea.

In my mind, I'm sitting in a field next to her, watching the sun drop over grassy Oklahoma farmland. I think that it must be lush and green, the opposite of everything here. She tells me she misses Flynn. I tell her I miss him too. She asks me about the day he died and I tell her. Her hand grazes mine, our eyes meet, our lips fit together, her tears are salty and hot; it feels right. Finally.

"Hey Marty," Flynn says. We are at opposite ends of the roof, our backs to each other. We have to almost yell.

"Yeah?"

"Sometimes it can be really nice out here you know? Sometimes it can be beautiful."

"You keep saying that. I still think you're fucked." He laughs; I feel my pulse quicken. "No, I mean it. You have so much at home. Oklahoma, your wife, your house. There's nothing worth a damn here. I don't get you."

He doesn't say anything and a while later we get relieved by two other marines. Downstairs, I remove my gear and begin spreading my sleeping bag over my sleeping mat. I hear his flak jacket drop from his body and hit next to his already made up sleeping space.

"Going out for a smoke," he says.

I turn to say I'll meet him, but he's already walking away. My eyes catch on his flak. A piece of dingy plastic is visible, just sticking up from the kangaroo pouch behind his magazines of ammunition. The note. My breath quickens, I look around for Flynn or the casual observer. There is no one, but still I do nothing.

I stare at it for some time before my grimy hand reaches to solidify its reality. I remove the plastic bag. Something so beautiful shouldn't be kept in such shoddy conditions, I think. My hand reaches inside the bag. The note warms my fingertips, as I slide it from its home. I bring it in front of my face, the white hurts my eyes it's so bright. I let it graze the stubble forming beneath my nostrils, breathing it in.

I smell nothing but the dirt and coppery stench of dried blood from my cracked hands. I unfold the paper, square by square, shaking. My vision begins to swim from holding my breath. I exhale, my eyes focus and I read:

Dear Daniel,

I can't do this anymore. I've met some one else. Some one who is there for me, and loves me, and wants me. His name is Troy Dowling. You remember him from high school. I'm leaving you, Danny. I'm sorry.

Jeanette

I read the note again. I flip the paper over, looking for the joke, but there isn't one. My head hurts. I feel cheated. I wish for horrible things to happen to Jeanette and her lover. I want to punish them. I want to make them beg forgiveness for what they've done. I want them to suffer for killing my hope. I can do nothing. I am eight thousand miles away in the middle of a war. The desert is shit. Home is shit. I fold the note carefully and return it to the pouch.

I try to remember how I got here. How I ended up so far from home.

I want to go back in time and tell that angry kid that no one back home will care. No one will throw themselves at his feet and beg him not to go. No one will write him long-winded letters about how things will be different when he comes home. I want to tell that kid not to do something stupid and spiteful.

He needs to know that it's not going to be medals and dress uniforms and John Wayne. It's not going to be bar girls from all over the globe and a party every night.

It's going to be shit, and no sleep, and dysentery, and dead friends. I want to tell him about the cheating wives, and the legless nightmares. And I want to tell him not to do it. But I can't.

Flynn sits on the concrete stoop, his cigarette smoked to the butt. I take a place beside my friend and offer him a smoke. The fallen night scoops us into the desert. I put my arm around him and tell him about Indiana, and why I never want to go back home.

The rain comes. Water slides down the stanchions on either side of the awning. Outside the walls of the widow's compound, dogs bark as the evening call to prayer sounds on distant loudspeakers atop minarets.

"It's beautiful tonight," I say.

Question for My Birth Mother
Colette Tennant

Looking past your swollen breasts,
your head bowed like a penitent praying,
did you ever give me a name?
When you washed dishes in the evening,
and my feet resisted your
big-belly push against the sink,
what name did you use to settle me?
At night, when I was spinning
like a rogue star in your belly,
did you launch a name into the black
universe of that one small room?
Did you give me a name
and do you remember it still,
you whose blood warms my fingers,
you whose heart kick-started mine?
You who held me nine months in darkness,
come to me in my most vivid dream,
divide the light from the darkness,
say my name, my very first name.

Deal Broken
Erick Mertz

Gets cold as vengeance up on the ridge. West of town, battered by the rough end of all weather that rolls our way. Of course, it's not much better in the valley on the streets of Monument neither. All us ranchers came to agreement on little regarding livelihood. Never was much consensus. We bickered often – at least, until this winter when the mule deer came down out of the hills and started cleaning out our stores of livestock feed. They seemed to get most everyone on the same track.

The law said we could shoot not even one of them deer on account of their herd already being thin. Population didn't seem thin to us. Seemed quite opposite, in fact. The Wildlife people said what we had was a local population problem. Called it an anomaly. Someone struck upon the idea that we'd simply draw them deer away from the ranches. We would pool a few bucks. We'd buy Darren Waltz' spare flatbed Ford and start bringing bales of alfalfa up to a feeding station we built together. Seemed easier than dragging on with a petition. I thought the deal was a good one. When Darren handed over the keys to his old rig, I thought it was a good enough thing we were doing. Everyone would kick in a bit and share the burden equally rather than risk getting cleaned out. So far that winter, the flatbed was our best plan.

It was a hard pill to swallow, figuring out how to tip-toe around a problem. Chore got to be custom though. Got to be that the men who went up on the ridge actually enjoyed each other's company. We'd go in pairs, knock back a rack of beer as we dropped a truckload of alfalfa for the herd that come down out of the woods at the sound of our approaching truck engine. Gentle creatures. Trusting. The chore was a chance to get to know your neighbor, someone who might only be a light on the far distant horizon, a name in the Bulletin or face across the diner. Most of us, while we didn't look forward to extra work, played along. Most of us made the best.

Most of us, that is, except Haney Cole.

Haney worked alone up on the ridge. The man lived alone and ate alone in town; he took no hand when it came to caring for his stock of animals. No rancher in Monument was about to force company on the ornery sort who refused the offer with hardly any hesitation. Better to let it be. Haney's shift fell in line after mine. I put off bringing him the truck for as long as I could on most mornings. Each visit to Haney's ranch ended up feeling like a confrontation. He'd press for information. He'd query on this and that. The old man was relentless to a fault, my wife would say.

When I got around to looking at the kitchen clock, I recognized that the day was on toward noon. He's still got to load the truck, I thought. Then he's got to drive it up the road, drop it and come back, all before nightfall. A fog was due to roll in. Ridge is already cold enough. Haney didn't deserve that ordeal, son of a bitch or not.

I pulled up through his old metal gate. The warning signs about trespass and illegal hunting clattered as the gate fell back, then I started to wind up through the series of blind switchbacks on the long hill toward his house. Haney lived on a bluff overlooking the valley, a few miles over from the ridge. He had a big house on a stretch of land, big enough that he could hardly walk from one end to the other without getting lost along the way. Haney built all of it himself when he moved into the county with his wife many years ago. Most who knew him as a young man said he was gentle. His first reputation was of being someone too soft for ranching life. Brought his new wife into town and told anyone who would listen about their plan. Never worked out though. No one quite knew the whole story on how or why, but Mrs. Cole left Monument and in the twenty-nine years since, no one went up that hill to replace her. Not even temporarily. There was enough in the way of speculation though. Coming up on his house it seemed to me that Haney was just some kid who never grew up.

His garage door was partially open. His dirt bike was out. It leaned against its kickstand in the wide gravel turnaround. As I pulled up to the front porch behind his rig, I lay into the truck horn, hopeful that he'd come out and take over the wheel. The old man was nowhere I could see though. I lay into the horn a few more times before giving up. The way we had our exchange worked out, I couldn't just drop the key; my truck was at the storehouse, all the way back down the hill, down the road in town. Haney was supposed to give me a ride to fetch it.

His house was dark. Curtains drawn. I walked down onto Haney's little side lawn but there was no sign of him there either. All that stood between the sky and me were a pile of old timbers for a play structure he'd planned on constructing long ago, overlooking grassland, then town further down. He dug four postholes but never bothered to fill them.

Around the corner, I spotted Haney in the silent depths of his workspace. He toiled in the shadows, dark coat blending his rigid figure in with a black, tar-paper background. He huddled over some project on his workbench, working in an awful hurry. It had always been my inclination to avoid disturbing anyone. As focused as Haney tended to be though, seemed like we both could have stood there all day.

"You hear me honk the horn?" I shouted.

Haney hardly glanced up: "Dean Durbin, I didn't even hear you there."

"I've got the truck around front if you're ready to go," I said. Haney tossed an oily rag into the shadows.

"Not going."

His back remained toward me, hands at his side.

"What are you talking about, Haney?"

"I am not going is what I said."

"What do you mean by that?" I laughed. "It's your turn."

The old man turned his weathered face toward me, hunting rifle in his hands.

"Not today, Dean," he said. "Told you twice. Will three times force the right impression?"

Haney threw the gun over his shoulder, pulling the army surplus strap so it fit tight against his body.

"Where you going with that?" I asked.

"Up to the feed station," he said. "Don't need the truck."

"How you getting up there?"

"I'm taking the motorbike."

"What exactly are you planning on?"

"Going to shoot a couple of them bucks," he said. I could hear the malice in his voice, clear as the morning sky. "Sons of bitches."

"I'd like to convince you otherwise," I said.

"We had a deal," Haney said.

"We have a deal," I said. "We have a deal with the others."

Haney shook his head adamantly as he ran a hand through his thick hair.

"Not like that, Dean. At least not how I see it."

"How do you see it then?"

"We had a deal with the damn deer."

Rummaging through a bin on the far end of his workbench, Haney found an old pair of mismatched gloves and a woolen ski mask to go over his face.

"I don't like your logic," I said. "At least come down to town and talk it out with the rest."

Haney grunted as he pulled the gloves on. The one for his left hand was too small. He had to force it over his chapped palm. When it was finally on, he stretched his leather-covered fingers, eyes flashing.

"Talk?" he roared, as though even after a brief meditation, that one particular word conveyed a unique quality of deception.

"Over coffee. Yes, talk. I'm sure everyone is sitting down at Doumit's right now, finishing up their lunch."

"Talk is what got us into this mess," he said. Haney looked around the garage. He was ready to go.

"Meaning?"

"Meaning, Dean," he said. "If you all would have just let me shoot six or nine of them deer in the first place."

"Then what?"

"Look, I'm out feed," he said. "Had a rough year to begin with. Then the whole herd come down the other night and ate my stock."

"Now you're done?"

He brushed past on his way to the motorbike. He threw one leg over the seat and got situated.

"Got to go. Can't be splitting hairs, especially after my mind is made."

"You go off like this," I said. "We're all going to share in the reckoning when the Wildlife people figure out what's transpired."

Haney pulled the mask down over his face as he kicked the bike to life.

"Don't worry, Dean. I know winter is hard on everyone. I don't intend on leaving any one of them deer up there to freeze. I'll bring back a piece for everyone."

The motorcycle roared to life as he slowly let out the throttle. It was well tuned. The bike was as eager to take on the road as its rider.

I waited, hopeful that he'd at least hesitate, but Haney took off out of the turnaround, gravel spraying off the back wheel as he spun up the road.

***

I crossed over the swollen creek on my way into town. Through the stoplight, I circled the block before finally pulling into Doumit's rear parking lot. I wondered whether anyone would question seeing the flatbed out in the afternoon, off of duty.

"You coming home soon?" my wife asked.

The phone booth overlooked the empty dining room. I watched the waitress bring a coffee serving and menu to the corner booth where I had dropped my coat.

"Soon," I replied. "At least I think."

The waitress returned to fill the white cup from a pot. She blotted a spill on the table with a rag from her apron before returning to her place folding napkins behind the counter.

"When exactly is soon, Dean?"

"I don't know," I said. "Can't quite say."

She sighed and hung up, asking no more questions.

I nursed my coffee while staring out the window. Midday was long past. Clouds were moving in. The winter sky was fast growing dark. My only companions were the Doumit's wait staff as they went through their afternoon shift change.

An hour had gone by when Brad Middleton came in from the cold. The doorbell rang. The waitress' attention turned suddenly as he ducked through the doorway. Brad was six foot ten inches tall, the only man in Monument who had to order each stitch of his clothing special. He was also a bachelor. He inherited the local tack and feed store from his uncle. Brad owned a ranch but he ran it more as a hobby. I felt a sense of relief as his stooped figure nodded in my direction while warming his bare hands near the radiator. Brad was decisive, sober in his thinking. I always found him to be downright fair when offering opinions.

"How you doing, Dean?" Brad asked.

He smiled and removed his yellow baseball cap.

"Good," I said as I indicated that he could join me in the booth. "How are you?"

"Coffee pot at the store is broken. Come down for a warm up," he said. "Is that the flatbed I saw parked out back?"

"Yes. It is."

The tack and feed store was off the main street. When Brad approached Doumit's, he came from the rear. I hadn't accounted for that as I searched for a discreet place to park the truck.

"Isn't it Haney's shift today though?"

The waitress arrived. She warmed my cup and brought a paper cup for Brad to take back to the store. I answered his question with a nod as she walked away.

"What did he do?" Brad asked.

"He went up to the ridge," I said. "But he didn't bring the feed truck."

"What did he bring then?"

"He brought his rifle."

Brad clutched the cup in his hands.

"His rifle?"

"Yes," I said. "Got on his motorcycle and took off. Quite determined too."

"Anyone else see him go?"

"Just me," I said.

Brad furrowed his long, narrow brow and took a sip off his coffee.

"Those deer must have gotten to his feed then?"

"Said something about that," I said. "At least he thinks they did."

Brad glanced at empty booths around the diner.

"I suppose there shouldn't be a problem," he said, quietly. "That is, unless it's you that goes and says something."

"I'm talking to you," I said. "That's all."

"What time did he head up?"

"About twelve-thirty."

"Oh well," Brad said. "Almost three o'clock now. What's done is done."

He stood up out of the booth and motioned to the kitchen.

"You take that with you," the waitress shouted from behind the counter. They exchanged flirtatious glances.

"Sure thing," he said. "I'll pay you ladies next time."

I was itching. Instead of waiting for his response, I asked him straight out: "What's right here, Brad?"

He stopped a few steps from the door then turned and looked directly at me.

"I don't know for sure," he said.

"We had a deal."

"Sure we did," he replied. "Deal is broken now though."

"Strikes me as wrong," I said.

Brad's hand went to the door. My gaze lowered.

"Right or wrong? None of us can say, maybe least of all those working at the Wildlife Bureau," Brad said. He sighed. "After all, what do they know?"

"But Brad, I'm telling you how it strikes me."

"I know you are. But I suppose, if Haney shares with the rest of us then no one really gets hurt."

*

The sun was down. Winter's bite filled the air as I stepped out of Doumit's.

I felt peculiar. My body was swimming from all the coffee. Lights were on up and down Front Street as I set to wandering. Those streetlamps still in operation bathed the empty sidewalk in a pale glow. Stretches of darkness filled in where the bulbs had burned out or been shattered by a .22 gauge.

I took one step off the sidewalk. My feet settled onto the uneven street. I looked all the way down to the vanishing point where Monument city limits ended. Beyond that, an untamed struggle for survival in the cold resumed.

I closed my eyes. Then I watched a house come to life up on the bluff. A porch light shining across the valley, pinprick piercing a silent fog, rolling in as called for in the evening forecast.

A mere pinprick of light, stubborn contrast to all that lay in its midst.

Work (Copland in the Woods)
John Byrne

Five bucks an hour, inside work,
No weeds (two bucks), no messy luncheon trays
(Three bucks); just write a press release or two
Each week – that's all I had to do:
This gallery will display ...
The theater troupe will stage this play ...
This orchestra premiers tomorrow night
The latest Copland work
And he, Oh God, is here
And I'm to transform five minutes of his time
Into eight paragraphs
When all the musicality I brought with me
Was Herman, Chad and Jeremy.
He took my cautious thrust:
"How do you decide what you'll write?"
With grace and led me to a forest walk,
Leaf strewn, sun speckled,
Quiet 'til his walking stick
Released two notes
Deep hidden in a fallen log
Encouraging a horde to fill his mind
Almost faster than he wrote them down.
I never did decide, he said,
Those notes decided me.
Unmusically, I typed away
To earn the precious bucks
Acknowledging he did the work
And I had all the luck.

If We Took a Deep Breath

Patty Somlo

The early morning clouds have nearly lifted and sun glints off the deep green water of the reservoir. Seeing the powerful grace of the Douglas firs that line the pathway as sunlight striking the water suddenly turns silver in the wind, I feel the low mood I've been carrying these last few days start to lift. It's odd, but I forget this feeling, until the moment I experience it. You see, to get to this place, I have to drive.

Unlike powering up a hillside on foot, I'm not accustomed to sitting behind the wheel of a car. Except for a handful of lessons that never kept me behind the wheel, I have only been driving the past year. This has nothing to do with any physical incapacity or my age. I am decades past the point of being old enough to get a license.

I can't help wondering if the people I pass walking their dogs, jogging, biking and even skateboarding, feel the way I do about this park. After 9/11, officials here in the City of Portland, Oregon created a stir when they proposed covering the park's three reservoirs, set here and there atop this long dormant volcano. Like the rest of the country, the city had become obsessed with terrorism, certain that Al-Qaeda had drawn up plans to poison our drinking water, stored in three historic stone reservoirs scattered throughout the park. A committee to save the reservoirs formed and a blizzard of studies were conducted, alternatives debated and hearings held. An overwhelming public response forced city officials to throw out every alternative but the status quo. Residents, it appeared, cared more about walking past their reservoirs than they feared Al-Qaeda would one day drop lethal chemicals into the water if the reservoirs were left uncovered.

Given all the high-profile targets Al-Qaeda could hit, our little neighborhood park seems an unlikely bet. I'm not even sure we're on any tourist must-see list. I study the water glittering in the small concrete pool and wonder how many times I've walked past it, noticing how the surface appears different, depending on the light. The park is covered with trees, some that change their leaves in the fall and flower in spring. Reflections slither across the reservoir, many days looking like a Monet painting still damp from the artist's brush. I'm always telling myself that next time I should bring my camera and photograph the water, then go back home and paint. Inevitably, I forget and have to remind myself all over again.

The park is just far enough away from my house that I need to drive. It's become a habit to take morning walks here, even in the rain, which is considerable once winter arrives. Part of my brain holds a fear deeper than any of these reservoirs that as soon as I press my foot down on the accelerator I will crash the car. Each morning, the fear argues with my mind's healthier side. The fear finds all sorts of excuses for why it's not a good idea for me to drive. At the start of the bout, I'm never sure which side of my brain will come out on top.

We're a long way from New York City here. An hour and a half's drive from town, you will find yourself on the sand, watching waves roll in from the Pacific. Greater than the physical distance, though, is the divide between our two ways of life. Unlike New York where it's best to look away from strangers, people passing on the sidewalk in Portland try to catch one another's gaze, then smile and say hi. It's okay to dine at a top restaurant in jeans, and some restaurant owners don't mind if you bring your dog. Etiquette on the bus requires you to thank the driver, even if you're stepping out the back door. So, maybe this explains our need for places to walk where we can see the reflections of trees and clouds. Instead of fear, maybe we're choosing life. It seems we aren't ready yet to give up the hope that looking one another in the eye will keep us safe.

To get myself to drive, I slip little reminders between the anxious thoughts of how much better I will feel when I reach the park. I tell myself it's good for me, like exercising when I'd rather curl up on the couch. If I don't drive, the dread will follow me all day, only to be replaced by a dark disappointment and shame. Once in a while when I'm being uncharacteristically kind to myself, I acknowledge that it's a miracle I've managed to drive well enough to buy my first car.

Like most bad habits, it's hard to trace the source of the fear. My unwanted attachment to fear grew slowly, from a small seed nourished over decades. Driving is not the only thing I grew up afraid to do but it's the one that's been hardest to overcome. In truth, I'm a nervous woman, worried about everything. Fear in my case is automatic. Like breath. I only notice the fear when it's not there.

Some mornings I walk past the middle reservoir glittering in the sun, under the awning of trees, up the wide road that's closed to cars, to the crest of the hill where a second smaller reservoir sits and whose water is the color of mud, and I marvel that anyone was silly enough to propose covering the key attractions in this park. While this might make me sound naïve, I'm not enough of a Pollyanna to believe that the folks who convinced a group of guys to hijack planes and fly them into skyscrapers aren't plotting new and more terrible deeds. It's just that covering up reservoirs in a small city park at the furthest edge of the continent seems a rather slight response. The water in these reservoirs is shallow, only four to six feet at their fullest. To combat terrorism, we need to go deep, to a place most Americans have not yet gone

As I walk uphill leaving the third reservoir behind and get a distant view of the steel and glass buildings downtown, I try a walking meditation I learned from a book by the Zen Buddhist master, Thich Nhat Hanh. On the in-breath, I remind myself to feel my fear, and on the out-breath, I let the fear out my partially opened lips, where it mingles with the air before vanishing. The meditation is a chant I repeat in time with my steps. Every time I practice this walking meditation, I am stunned by the results. Instead of the anxious thoughts that normally prowl around my head, colliding with one another as they compete for my attention, the meditation acts like a quiet mountain stream, clearing the debris along its path. Suddenly, I notice the light on the trees, a robin I wouldn't have seen, a branch backlit by the sun. I realize I am more than the fear that too often leaves me running in place, on a track so worn from my footsteps, I feel as if I've sunk too deep to escape.

Usually, I spend part of my walking time worrying about the drive I have to make to get back home. I even trace the route in my mind, visualizing all the places I might crash. The walking meditation gives me a break, the way a massage does, leaving me little choice but to relax.

Ten years after 9/11, I admit that I still can't comprehend what fuels the rage and fervent belief that pushes so many young men to want to kill Americans and Europeans, and take their own lives in the process. When I read about more futures snuffed out by bombs strapped around someone's waist or carried in a backpack where books should have been resting, I realize that there's a world of people, furious because they believe we have robbed them of their space. And I wonder what might happen if we all took a deep breath, then smiled at the bombers and said, "Can you please move back a little and we'll let you have the space?"

The last part of the climb is the hardest. I've done the hike enough, so I at least know it's short. On a clear day, you can look east and see Mt. Hood's snow-covered top at one particular spot. The snow on Mt. Hood turns a pale rose close to sunset.

Just down the hill another clearing in the trees provides a glimpse of the foothills stacked one in front of the next, like dark volumes on a shelf. If I'm feeling especially anxious or low, that view, more than the one of glorious Mt. Hood, will cheer me up. I'm not sure why, but I suspect it's because the view is of infinity. I can't see where the foothills end. Being able to see a distance as long as forever causes me to feel that hope is not lost.

As I begin the descent, I think, as I often do, that fear is a cancer, swallowing up everything bright and happy and brave and hopeful in its path. The only way to stop it is by going directly to the source. For a lot of reasons, I grew up feeling helpless, a victim rather than an actor in my life. Every time I drive, I take a tiny bit of power from that car and pour it into my life. Eventually, I know, I will be powerful enough to win any bout my fear proposes.

I reach the lower reservoir and end my walk, by circling around the narrow pathway once. Rather than covering up the reservoirs to keep us safe, the city chose to hire security guards, and they patrol the park on bikes. In Portland, known for its green philosophy, where more than a quarter of its residents commute to work by bike, this seems an appropriate response. The guard rounds the bend pedaling slowly, as I come around. He is wearing a bright yellow nylon bike shirt on which he's attached his badge.

In moments, I step off the pavement onto the grass to let him ride by. As he peddles past, he makes sure to look me straight in the eye.

Close the Door
Mary Arana

I sometimes close the door as the last of my fourth-graders arrive, shut out thoughts of their lives outside and see only our world in the classroom.

Never mind her tangled hair, dirt-scuffed sleeves and chewed fingernails.

Never mind he draws swastikas in the back of his notebook; tracing the outlines of the older brother he wants to be.

Never mind that she shoves yet another student and glowers over her recovered marker.

Never mind the rattling slam of the classroom door, his head jolting back in to yell, "I'll see you all in Juvie!"

Never mind her downcast eyes, soft voice whispering that her family moved to a homeless shelter.

Instead, I turn to build our shared cocoon—rain streaking against the glass windows, our eyes on each other and the life we create with our pencils, books and broken crayons.

Math: each fumbled number picked up again and restored to sense, placed in logical, predictable context.

Author's Circle: raised hands wave to offer comments to half-formed ideas.

Reading: decoded words cast into stories of fantasy and promise of what will one day come.

Recess: cliques form and harden.

Lunchtime: trays spill.

It will not always be like this. My voice parses strategies for double-digit multiplication, and their voices singsong the chant back to me again.

You can have a different kind of life. The document camera picks up the image of my hand, enlarging it dramatically across the screen. He grips his own pencil and copies, constructing the outline for an essay.

Who you are is priceless. She bites her lip in concentration, drawing a circular arrowthrough her poster, marking out the life cycle of a frog.

Your culture, challenges, and dreams each stand ready. Twenty-nine fourth-graders hunch under their backpacks and press against the classroom door; waiting for the bell's release to return home.

I see you, I whisper as my last student bolts toward the bus, worn sneakers squeaking against the wet pavement—one glance cast back over her shoulder.

Remnants litter the floor: dropped notes, pencil shavings, half-finished assignments. The pieces they've been given by parents, community and previous generations; these are theirs alone to interweave and form anew.

Rhosymedre

Amy Miller

We were so unlovely. We butchered our bows
on your crescendos. Our fingers pawed
the backward strings, drunken pizzicatos
clattered the lanes of your quiet town.
The hymn broke through,
violas parting wild ground
like the plows of heavy horses,
turning up a skeleton of you
with your sharped C's
and switchback scales. How it looked
so simple—whole measures
on a single string—but then the violence
of pursuit, cellos bucking their separate arcs,
half the violins stalling in air.
Still, I heard you. You hummed
the phrases of my middle ear, sang
the theme of my short drive home,
love's face gone from the dark window
of the night café, a dog's bright collar
dancing your diminuendo in the crosswalk.

"Rhosymedre" ("Lovely"): a song adapted by
Ralph Vaughan Williams for "Three Preludes on
Welsh Hymn Tunes," now a staple of small orchestras

Risk Management
Marc Janssen

Just in case it begins to gently rain
Just in case the head is separated
Just in case one shirt sleeve is longer
Just in case I forget what day it is
Just in case the front door lock is busted
Just in case dead fish blacken the stream bed
Just in case hydrogen is flammable
Just in case clients start to show remorse
Just in case someone loses some money
We will do nothing, do nothing, nothing

Suffrage Poems

Suffrage Poems
An Interview with Mike Chasar

Tell us a little about your background and how you became involved with these Suffrage Poems.

My research focuses on the history and culture of American popular poetry—verse in all forms as it appeared or appears (take a big breath) in newspapers, periodicals, scrapbooks, advertisements, and movies; on the radio, television, and billboards; and on all sorts of consumer objects ranging from greeting cards to candy boxes, pin-up posters, and pillow shams. Some of this verse is "literary," and some of it (like advertising poetry) does not appear to have much literary pretension, but most of it intersects with mass culture or people's everyday lives in surprising and complex ways.

When I started teaching at Willamette in 2009, I wanted my research and teaching to tap into the history of popular poetry in the Northwest in some way. So when I discovered the poetry printed in every issue of the *New Northwest*—I first heard about the early women's rights paper from a docent wearing period attire and in character as a pioneer wife at the High Desert Museum in Bend—I ran with it. A fair amount was written by people living in Salem and the Willamette Valley before Washington, Idaho, Montana and Wyoming were states (the paper ran from 1871 to 1887), and the paper appears to have cultivated and sustained a literary community in this area long before people like William Stafford, Theodore Roethke, and Richard Hugo helped put the Northwest on the national literary map. So, because it's been forgotten, because the poetry appeared to be so important to the paper's goal of women's suffrage, and because many narratives of literary history in the Northwest depict the nineteenth century as a dismal period of literary production best forgotten, I figured that there was a lot to be learned from it—and there is!

What was the historical atmosphere during the time these were written?

These poems are part of the long wind-up to the Progressive Era in U.S. history—a period of major political activism in both states and territories that resulted in reforms having to do with women's rights, labor (including child labor), temperance, living conditions in urban centers, truth in advertising, education, corporate practices, and so on. Oftentimes in response to the excess, opulence, and laissez-faire economic practices of the Gilded Age's "one percent," Progressive Era efforts resulted in things like the income tax, compulsory schooling laws, the passage of the Pure Food and Drug Act, muckraking literature like Upton Sinclair's The Jungle, Prohibition, women's suffrage, urban sanitation systems and housing reforms, the National Park system, and government regulation of big business.

When we hear "Progressive Era" today, it's oftentimes used pejoratively on Fox News, where commentators see it as the first major movement in U.S. history establishing "Big Government" practices that do supposedly un-American things at the federal level like regulate child labor, limit the work week to forty hours, pursue the administration of civil rights, federalize land, tax for the purposes of setting up public sanitation systems, schools, roads, and so on. And Fox News isn't wrong: there's a direct link between the ethical motivations, social justice imperatives, and religious impulses of the Progressive Era to things like Obamacare, efforts to raise taxes on the wealthy, and environmental justice today. Barack Obama comes out of a Progressive Era tradition, Mitt Romney from a tradition that governed during the Gilded Age.

The poetry world of the 1870s and 1880s was complicated too. American readers revered a set of five New England poets known as the Fireside Poets or Schoolroom Poets (William Cullen Bryant, Oliver Wendell Holmes, Henry Wadsworth Longfellow, James Russell Lowell, John Greenleaf Whittier and sometimes Ralph Waldo Emerson). It's hard to understate the power these poets had on American literary life—in publishing, education, and in promoting or celebrating a set of conservative religious, agrarian, anti-modern, and literary values. They were so revered that group portraits of them were mass produced and sold to hang over fireplaces in American homes nationwide! As America's first crop of home bred poets, they were an amazing phenomenon, but by the 1870s and 1880s they were getting old. Bryant died in 1878, Longfellow and Emerson in 1882, Lowell in 1891, Whittier in 1892, and Holmes in 1894. Add to that Ralph Waldo Emerson's death in 1882, and you have what Charles Bernstein would call an "official verse culture" that was aging, generally resistant to the forces of change and modernity or else just simply out of touch, and lots of young poets trying to figure out how to get beyond the artistic and cultural precedent they set.

What we call "Modernism" or the New Poetries would eventually do that in the 1910s and 1920s, reconstituting a new official verse culture—more or less the one we've inherited today—replete with little magazines, official prizes (like the Pulitzer), and organizations like the Poetry Society of America.

At the same time, there was a wealth of poetry being written and read outside of nineteenth-century official verse culture and before the New Poetries as well. A lot of this poetry, as the *New Northwest* suggests, was political or ephemeral in nature. Advertisements were loaded—totally loaded—with poetry of all types. People with disabilities sold poems on the streets to raise money. Readers kept scrapbooks full of poems they wanted to save or share. Civic events included poems. Newsboys made extra money by writing and delivering poems called "carrier's addresses" at New Year. In the absence of television and movies, families read poems together—or saw them illustrated with magic lantern slide performances. There was a thriving world of what we might call amateur writing and reading that has by and large not been studied but that we sort of intuit in our cultural bones was there. The same thriving world of popular verse is the case with the twentieth century too—though it strikes us as far less intuitive, I think, to imagine poetry proliferating in the twentieth century rather than disappearing; that's why my book *Everyday Reading* sets out to study popular poetry in modern America, in particular, rather than in the nineteenth century.

Tell us about the journey of finding the poems.

When I first looked at the *New Northwest*—on microfilm, before it was digitized as part of the Historic Oregon Newspapers initiative—there were more poems than I knew what to do with: over fifteen years of weekly newspapers, some issues with five or six poems printed in them. Unlike some of the prose in the paper—such as the editorials and serialized novels written by the paper's editor and Oregon's leading suffragette Abigail Scott Duniway—no one, so far as I can tell, has studied, collected, or even read with a mote of seriousness the poetry, even though the paper regularly placed poems prominently on page one.

Knowing I wanted to work with the poems but that collecting and reading them—and also reading the paper to get a sense of the context in which they appeared—would be a lengthy process, I made it part of a "Poetry of the Pacific Northwest" class that I teach. Each student is assigned to find, transcribe, edit, and present poems from ten issues of the paper along with notes on relevant news items and other content. Then we read those poems as a group, both to get a sense of the poetry broadly—topics, themes, styles, etc.—and to analyze them individually. Recovering an archive like this can be hard and tedious work, and every semester we have to learn how to read them on their own terms assuming that, at one point in time, they were important and appealing to readers, and then trying to figure out why.

Why did you and your class decide to pick these poems?

In addition to studying the poems, the most recent instantiation of "Poetry of the Pacific Northwest" also partnered with an experimental scriptwriting class in the Theater Department that wanted to create a play about the history and legacy of women's suffrage in Oregon—as one way to mark and commemorate 2012 as the one hundredth anniversary of Oregon women's suffrage. (See Century of Action: Oregon Women Vote 1912-2012 for other such events.) As part of the experimental nature of the script, the class thought it would be cool to start with a bunch of poems from the *New Northwest*, using them as raw material to collage, break up, or interlace through the script in funky and innovative ways. It can sometimes be difficult to figure out what to "do" with archival materials other than, well, archive them and study them; so we thought it would be interesting to motivate them in another way, too—toward the creation of a new piece of art. From what I understand, the script is still in progress, but the plan is to give it a full production at the university in early 2013!

So, our first goal was to select poems to present to that class, and toward that end we had two main priorities: 1) select poems that surveyed the different types of arguments being made at the time for extending the vote to women; and 2) select poems with varying poetic strategies, rhetorical components, and performance possibilities. We thought the former would gesture to some of the political complexities of that historical moment that get lost in a debate framed simply as "for" or "against" women's suffrage. (As with the debate about healthcare today, people aren't just for or against it, but have different reasons for being for or against it, or partly for it and partly against it—you get the idea.) And we thought the latter would shine a light on the diversity of styles and poetic techniques of popular verse, which oftentimes gets characterized as entirely "sentimental" and generally homogenous in style, format, rhetoric, etc.; in actuality, the poetry is pretty diverse—song lyrics, persona poems, narrative poems, lyric poems, satire, dialect, etc.—so we wanted to honor that aspect of the writing.

I made the selections for Gold Man keeping these two elements in mind as well, so that we have inspirational song lyrics ("Campaign Song"), two very different dramatic monologues that make different arguments about women and the vote ("The Perplexed Housekeeper" and "'Siah's Vote"), a serious narrative with children as main characters ("Reasons"), a humorous narrative ("Wife Versus Horse"), a romance ("Katie Lee and Willie Grey"), and a lyrical extended metaphor ("My Ship"). In addition to the generic diversity—all are totally part of a culture of poetry that lent itself to oral delivery or performance—the poems also make a pretty wide variety of arguments for how and why women should get the vote: "The Perplexed Housekeeper" suggests that women are already excellent multi-taskers and won't be burdened with one more thing to do; "'Siah's Vote" argues that women already participate in voting via the advice they give to their men-folk; "Campaign Song" says women will help clean up a corrupted culture of voting but also makes the problematic claim that "John Chinaman" can now do the work once done by women and thus free women up for public life; and "The Ship" shows us a character abandoned and forlorn because what must be the "ship of state" mentioned in Duniway's poem never comes for her. That's just a quick overview, but you get the idea: poets are using different poetic strategies to make different types of arguments about the political enfranchisement or disenfranchisement of women.

What does women's "suffrage" mean, for those who are unfamiliar with the term?

Today, "suffrage" is a noun meaning "the collective vote of a body of persons," so that we speak of "women's suffrage," "African American suffrage," "universal suffrage," and so on. According to the *Oxford English Dictionary*, the term was first used in the fourteenth century to refer to religious intercessions, petitions, or prayers for the dead. It appears that the plea for help or support in these prayers got abstracted from church con-texts to generally refer to help or assistance, so that voting "suffrage" refers to the assistance requested of a group of people in making a decision—like choosing a candidate for office.

What was suffrage and when did it happen?

Women's suffrage happened at different points in time in different places and at different levels of government or social organization (national, state, local, school, etc.), so that in the nineteenth century some women were allowed to vote on certain matters in one city or state but not in another; and sometimes some women were allowed to vote while others were not (white women, for example, were sometimes enfranchised before women of color, and sometimes the fight for women's suffrage was divided from within by people who didn't think suffrage should be extended to non-white American women). To get a partial sense of how complicated this history is, think of the much shorter history of the fight for gay marriage rights: some states honor "civil unions" and some don't; some states marry people of the same sex, some don't; some churches perform unions, some don't; and some states or churches or levels of government or even individual businesses may or may not recognize the marital status confirmed on someone somewhere else.

In Oregon, for example, some women—lawmakers specified "women who are widows, and have children and taxable property in the district"—were allowed to vote in school elections in 1862, probably because those women had no men who could otherwise represent them. In 1878, that language, but still only for voting in school elections, was expanded to include any women over the age of twenty-one who owned property. Oregon placed the question of women's suffrage at the state level on the ballot six times (1884, 1900, 1906, 1908, 1910, and 1912); sometimes the legislature passed the measure but it was voted down by voters. In November, 1912, Oregon voters approved women's suffrage by 52 percent, but even then not all Oregon women could vote: first-generation immigrant women and most Native American women weren't allowed to vote because until 1924 they weren't allowed to become U.S. citizens. The nineteenth amendment to the U.S. Constitution was ratified in 1920, extending to all American women who were considered citizens the right to vote regardless of the state in which they lived. (For much better histories, from which I'm cribbing these figures, check out the "Woman Suffrage in Oregon" entry on the Oregon Encyclopedia or the materials made available at the Century of Action web site.)

Can you briefly explain the time in history, the state of the country, Oregon, popular writers/poets at the time, etc.?

Even though I've drawn comparisons between the last three decades of the nineteenth century and the current day, it's important to remember that American life was very different then. When Duniway began publishing the *New Northwest*, Oregon had been a state for twelve years, and the Civil War had been over for just six years. The U.S. military was occupying the South (which it would do until 1877, ending Reconstruction and ushering in the age of Jim Crow laws, the KKK, and regular lynching of African Americans). In 1871, the first-ever photos of Yellowstone were taken, the first Major League Baseball game was played, and the Great Chicago Fire burned for three days destroying over three square miles of the city. And Mark Twain wouldn't start working in earnest on *The Adventures of Huckleberry Finn* for another five years. At the time, there was no television, electricity, telephone, phonograph, automobile, radio, system of paved roadways, or antibiotics. Daily papers and books were printed on the letterpress. People made soap at home, entertained themselves with magic lanterns and stereoscopes, singing with family, reading aloud, scrapbooking and lectures. They traveled by stagecoach and, increasingly, by railroad (the first transcontinental route was finished in 1869).

In 1871, about 90,000 people—53,000 men and 37,000 women—lived in the entire state of Oregon, including about 1,200 people in Salem and 8,200 in Portland. The census of 1870 reported fewer than 350 African Americans in Oregon (when Oregon became a state, it was as a free state, but it did not permit African American residents). There were over 3,300 documented Chinese workers, and they faced brutal work conditions, violence, and serious discrimination such as the Sunset Laws in Pendleton, which prohibited any person of Chinese origin from being above ground after sunset, and, later, the Chinese Exclusion Act of 1882. By the 1870s, most native or First Nations peoples had been removed to reservations, and with the end of the treaty system in 1871 were no longer treated as sovereign. Average life expectancy in the U.S. was in the mid 40s with only two or three percent making it to 65. On average, women had seven or eight live births; figures from Boston report that twenty percent of children in that city died before the age of one and that thirty-five percent of children died before age five. In Chicago, 62% of all deaths were children under age five. I can't imagine the figures were much different for Oregon. Not a very pretty picture, is it?

No doubt many women wrote for the same range of reasons that people write today—to contribute to public discourse, for entertainment, for the possibilities of self-expression and empowerment, for the love of language and narrative, to be part of a writing scene or community—but I think the stakes of their writing and publishing were much higher than they would be for most American women writing today. The dominant philosophy of gender roles at this time was what we now call the "separate spheres" ideology, which assigned to men the responsibilities of public life (including voting and governance) and to women the responsibilities of home life (housework, religion, care and education of children, etc.). Men were supposed to deal with the vagaries and dirtiness of daily life and practical affairs like money and policy, while women were portrayed as the nation's conscience and thus embodied a "selfless" corrective to men's work that needed to stay unsullied and somehow pure; a common way of imagining this ideal was as the "Angel in the House." Insofar as the separate spheres ideology discouraged and even prohibited women's voices in public, it would have been quite a risky endeavor for women not just to write, but then publish, these poems. At the same time, in a discourse that would be called "Republican motherhood," these various qualities became some of the more prominent arguments for extending women the right to vote, insofar as women—so the argument went—would inject the values of moderation, temperance, religion, and education into the corrupted political sphere of greed, alcoholism, war and business; who better to care for a nation than the selfless, religious mother?

Some of the risks of publishing are visible in the poems' bylines alone—some are published anonymously, sometimes they use pen names, sometimes they include just a first name—that protect their writers from the ramifications of speaking in public while allowing them a voice at the same time. But different types of poems had different stakes as well: poems about children, religion, morality, temperance, nature and the like would have been more acceptable, even encouraged, than poems about voting or other issues of public policy. Thus, one of the things that continues to interest me is how some of these poets manage to turn more acceptable topics and approaches into poems about voting. Take a poem like "The Ship," for example, where Florence Percy (the pen name of Elizabeth Akers Allen, a real-life writer from New England) shows us the devotion, loyalty and heartbreak of a woman going to the docks everyday and waiting—a conceit that readers would have readily associated with wives of fishermen, sailors, etc.—for "my ship" to come in. But in Percy's case—and especially printed in the pages of the *New Northwest*—that ship, even as it's not given specific meaning, signifies as the Ship of State, not as a lover or husband or brother. While some writers, like Duniway, addressed the subject of suffrage directly, many others did so indirectly, playing to social expectations only to subvert them. This aspect of the writing asks us to re-read poems that don't initially strike us as "political," much less complex, for any number of subtexts, associations, implications, or ironies that link them to politics.

What should readers look for and appreciate about these poems?

Because the poems are heavily metered and rhyming, they can strike a modern ear as sounding limited in range or scope, but as I suggested earlier, they're really pretty diverse, cultivating different arguments for women's suffrage and employing different techniques of narrative, humor, speaking voice, and the like. They were written in and for a culture that read poems out loud, as well, so they also display highly performance-oriented aspects of repetition, pathos, and clearly defined personae that are different from many of the first-person based, free-verse lyric poems we see in magazines and journals today.

So, as you read them, remember that you're reading these poems in a modern medium—the so-called "little magazine"—that didn't exist back then and that is designed and printed with technologies that weren't available, if even imaginable, back then either. You're likely reading them via an electric light that wouldn't have existed, with more education than readers in 1871 would have had, and you're probably reading them alone and in private rather than in a family setting. You're reading them in a culture where women speaking about politics is not as dangerous, in a state where women have had the right to vote for a century now, and in an age when poems aren't part of the daily newspaper and when the newspaper itself—once a medium that dominated U.S. life—is on the verge of disappearing.

Try, then, to take yourself back to the state of Oregon in 1871. You're one of 1,200 people in Salem, you've just watered the horses or put the wagon in the barn, and it's growing dark so you need to light the oil lamp. Your family comes home; the kids use the outhouse, and instead of going to their respective rooms to play video games (indeed, there likely aren't separate rooms for every member of the family or even for sleeping), they pick up the sewing or homework, stoke the fire, and gather together. If things are going well, your husband isn't drunk on the town square; instead, to ward off the chill, he takes a sip of the alcohol-based patent medicine he bought from a traveling nostrum salesman. There is a fire burning in Chicago—it will burn for three days and go down in history as one of the largest disasters to ever strike an American city—but you won't hear about it that night or the next. Instead, you pick up the *New Northwest*, the new newspaper started by the Scott girl, which you read for its mixture of news, ads, advice, poems, and ripping good serialized stories. Her personal story, you reflect, is perhaps not so different than your own, as she came West from Illinois in a party of thirty people and five ox-drawn wagons in 1852; both her mother (of cholera) and her three year-old brother died along the way. Seventeen at the time, she'd since married a farmer and had six children, taught school, and ran a women's accessories shop down in Albany. Now, at age 37, her husband Benjamin permanently disabled as a result of an accident involving a runaway team of horses, Abigail has moved to Portland, started a paper, and is writing and speaking—with her husband's support—about the vote. What a woman, you think.

Then you look down at the paper and discover that someone you know—Mrs. F.D. Gage, let's say—has written a poem about all of the work housewives do, referring to herself as "wife, mother, nurse, seamstress, cook, housekeeper, chambermaid, laundress, dairywoman and scrub." Chambermaid? Laundress? Scrub? You read it to yourself with some shock and wonder, and then, when the kids get sent to bed, you read it to your spouse. What could this lead to next?

Campaign Song

Mrs. A.J. Duniway
The New Northwest, 8 Sept 1871

Hail to the brightly dawning day
    When the glorious Ship of State,
With men and women all embarked
    To meet their coming fate,
Shall navigate the ship, my friends,
    Where politicians play,
For they've taken a trip in the Government ship
    And sadly gone astray.

CHORUS

Then blow ye winds a-ho, a-voting we will go;
We'll stay no more on the barren shore,
But hand in hand with brothers band,
        We'll guide the Ship of State
          Across the raging main
      Of Governmental seas, my friends,
        To meet our coming fate.

Good-bye, good-bye to the whisky rings;
    Good-bye to Government broils;
No more shall men with vote and pen
    Appropriate the spoils;
For we'll navigate the Ship of State
    Beside our Brothers dear,
And when the breakers round us dash
    We'll shun 'em – never fear.

CHORUS

Good-bye, good-bye to service work

Where wages are not known;
John Chinaman is here to wash
    And sew your buttons on.
He'll cook your beefsteak too, my boys,
    And darn your stockings well,
While we, like you, will legislate
    And trade and buy and sell.

CHORUS

We'll keep the fireside too, my boys,
    And read your musty tomes;
We'll use the money that we earn
    To beautify your homes;
We'll use the wisdom we acquire
    To legislate for good;
We know that with our cause you'll stand
    When we are understood.

Reasons

Mrs. Ajax

18 July 1873

A True Story

One night, after tea, Master Johnny and Sue
Sat down at the table their problems to do.

Their task was in Euclid, and just about where
The circle they wished t'inscribe in a square.

Both eager began the two lines to draw,
And when the whole thing little Sue thought she saw,

"My string's in a knot!" baby cries with a shout.
"Quick, Susie, my darling, help clear his snarls out,"

Said the mother's kind voice; so what should she do,
But leave mathematics, and cope with the shoe.

One moment, no more! Then, back to her book,
O'er the points once gained, again she must look.

Meantime, unmolested, her dear brother John,
The first problem finished, the next plodded on.

Quick as flash Susie worked; the circle inscribed;
And scarcely the new proposition had tried,

When again spoke the mother: "It comes to my mind
That Johnnie's blue coat wants a button behind.

"He can't go to school without it, you know;
Come, Susie, my dear, please let the book go!

"'Twill take but a second, with fingers so nimble;
Then jump up, my child, get your scissors and thimble.

"There, that's a bright girl! and now run along!
But first, be quite sure you fasten it strong."

This one she made fast; but alas! for the thread
Just lost in her book, it had slipped from her head.

Again she reviewed; worked rapid and well,
Though oft called away; indeed, I can't tell

The number of times that this sister Sue
Was summoned by all, "little nothings" to do.

When, interrupted, Johnny sat, feeling sad
That a sister so careless of study he had.

Till, his lessons all learned, he sprang from the table,
With an air that savored of—"We boys are able."

Now, the house being still, and the hour being late,
Susie studies, content that such is her fate.

When the door opens quick, her father steps in:
"How could I let Sue these branches begin!

"John's work is accomplished, and he gone to bed;
But you can't give a girl a boy's clearer head!",

Sue heard the remark, and she thought a reply,
But couldn't quite make it, and good reason why.

She thought if she queried why John didn't stay,
And sew on the buttons burst off in his play,

Or why baby's tangles he couldn't clear out,
Or help, now and then, in the running about—

In short, if she said all the things she could say,
Woman's rights there would be, if no other, to pay.

But, next day, at school, at the head of her class—
Ahead of each boy, and ahead of each lass—

Up stood little Sue, and her points proved as clear,
As though she had studied for many a year.

Both shoulders Johnny shrugged, and said with a grin:
"Yet girls are no students; they glance and take in
The whole of a theme, ere the 'great minds' begin.

"'"Siah's Vote"

Anonymous
3 May 1872

What a silly lot of fellows!
      Mind, you don't repeat a word!
Raising such a noise and rumpus,
      If a woman's voice is heard!
Bless me, don't they talk in meeting!
      Can't they pray and talk a way—
Talk, according to my notion,
      Good as men do any day?

Foolish men! we're voting always;
      Kinder sly, but voting still.
There's my 'Siah—he's contented,
      Cause he thinks he has his will;
But, la! Bless me, when 'tis 'lection,
      Don't he always come to me,
Asking who he'd better vote for?
      So he votes for me, you see.

Now I have a kind of notion,
      I'm not rich or larned: but then,
All this talk and great commotion
      Comes from just this kind of men;
Like my 'Siah, he's fond of reading,
      But he'd rather hold the plough;
So I read and tell him of it—
      That's the way most men vote now.

'Siah comes in to supper hungry,
      So he asks me "what's to pay?"
Then I sit and tell him mostly
      What I've read 'twixt whiles all day,

'Lection times he says, "You settle
        On the names you like the best;
Pick out men of pluck and mettle—
        I'll attend to all the rest."

Now it seems to me if 'Siah
        Don't keep posted, and I do,
I'm the one to do the voting—
        Neighbor, how it looks to you?
There's my doctor, he can't read none—
        Patients running night and day;
But his wife she reads it for him—
        She's the voter, I should say.

There's my marm in Sleepy Hollow,
        Pays more taxes twice than 'Siah;
Marm's an awful team for working,
        Can't no men folks come a-nigh her.
All her darkies vote; but marm, sir,
        She can work just like man,
Mind the laws, but never make them,
        Pay big taxes and be calm.

"Take it home, how would you like it?"
        So you said about the slave;
Tell you what, when women vote, sir,
        They'll vote honestly and brave;
Won't catch woman shirking voting,—
        Catch her voting for a scamp!
No, sir! when we get to voting,
        Drunkards, rascals, thieves will tramp.

'Siah, he would vote with me, sir!
        'Siah's sister, like her man;
It would all come out just right, sir—
        Takes a woman's head to plan.
"Vote for you, sir, when we get it?"
        Not if I can keep my mind!
Can't buy women's votes just yet, sir—
        Women voters ain't that kind.

No, sir! if I do lack larning,
        I can teach the boys and 'Siah
How to vote at our town meeting;
        Other women can look higher,
But I ask, and stick to asking,
        If I know enough to tell
Other folks just how to vote, sir,
        Can't I vote, myself, as well?

Wife Versus Horse

[Author unknown]
21 February 1873

"Bless me," said stout Guy Harndon,
    "My precious blooded mare
Has coughed three times to-day, wife;
    There's something wrong, I swear."
Straight to the doctor went he,
    And bustling in, exclaimed:
"Come, doctor, come see Topsy."
    "Ah, Topsy, is she lamed?"
"Lamed, no, but coughs some, doctor;
    'Tis nothin' much, as yet,
But men are rather skittish
    When colds seize on a pet."

Away went man and doctor;
    And in the stable warm
They closed and petted Topsy,
    Lest she might come to harm.
For weeks they watch her kindly,
    For weeks her food prepare;
Blanket, and [illegible] and bedding—
    She has the best of care.
But in the house, sick, lonely,
    Lies Harndon's wife the while;
No one to speak to her kindly,
    Uncheered by friendly smile.

"You sick?" says Guy, on seeing
    Her nestled in the bed;
"Confound these women, grunting
    With snuffles in the head!
Stir round, that's what you need, child;
    Rouse up, and work a spell;

Take my advice, 'tis work, Jen,
    That keeps a woman well."

Now "Jen," that very morning,
    Had cleaned his Sunday coat,
Mended his precious gauntlets,
    Made neckties for his throat,
Prepared a fav'rite pudding,
    Rocked baby for an hour;
And then poor Jenny Harndon
    Found work beyond her power.

Down stairs stalked stout Guy Harndon,
    Scolding his boy and girl,
And on, out through the kitchen
    He strode, in angry whirl;
"Confound these women's fancies!
    I wanted her to see
If Topsy's looks had changed much,
    But there she is, you see."

I stood by stout Guy Harndon,
    And, as I watched him well,
I asked myself this question—
    The answer who can tell?—
What was it this Guy Harndon
    Promised, one autumn day
To love and cherish? horses,
    Or little Jennie Gray?
                    —[Woman's Journal].

Katie Lee and Willie Grey

Margaret Verne

15 March 1872

Two brown hands tossing curls,
Red lips pouting over pearls,
Bare feet white and red with dew,
Two eyes black and two eyes blue—
Little boy and little girl were they—
Katie Lee and Willie Grey.

They were standing where a brook,
Bending like a shepherd's crook,
Flashed its silver, and thick ranks
Of green willow lined its banks,
Half in sport and half in play—
Katie Lee and Willie Grey.

They had cheeks like berries red;
He was taller—'most a head;
She, with arms like wreaths of snow,
Swung a basket to and fro,
As she loitered, half in play,
Chattering to Willie Grey.

"Pretty Katie," Willie said,
And then came a blush of red
Through the brownness of his cheek—
"Boys are strong and girls are weak,
And I will carry, so I will
Katie's basket up the hill."

Katie answered with a laugh,
"You shall carry only half;"
And then pushing back her curls,

"Boys are weak as well as girls."
Do you think that Katie guessed
Half the wisdom she expressed?

Men are only boys grown tall—
Hearts don't change much, after all.
And when, long years from that day,
Katie Lee and Willie Grey
Stood again beside the brook,
Bending like a shepherd's crook,

It is strange that Willie said—
While again a dash of red
Crossed the brownness of his cheek—
"I am strong and you are weak;
Life is but a slippery steep
Hung with shadows cold and deep;

Will you trust me, Katie dear,
Walk beside me without fear?
May I carry, if I will,
All your burdens up the hill?"
And she answered, with a laugh,
"No, but you may carry half!"

Close beside the little brook,
Bending like a shepherd's crook,
Washing, with its silver hands,
All day long the pearly sands,
Is a cottage where to-day
Katie lives with Willie Grey.

My Ship

Florence Percy (pseudonym of Elizabeth Akers Allen)
1 March 1872

Down to the wharves, as the sun goes down,
    And the daylight's tumult and dust and din
Is dying away in the busy town,
    I go to see if my ship comes in.

I gaze far over the quiet sea,
    Rosy with sunset, like mellow wine,
Where ships, like lilies, lie tranquilly,
    Many and fair,—but I see not mine.

I question the sailors every night,
    Who over the bulwarks idly lean,
Noting the sails as they come in sight,—
    "Have you seen my beautiful ship come in?"

"Whence does she come?" they ask of me;
    "Who is her master, and what her name?"
And they smile upon me pityingly
    When my answer is ever and ever the same.

O, mine was a vessel of strength and truth:
    Her sails were white as a young lamb's fleece;
She sailed, long since, from the port of south—
    Her master was Love and her name was Peace.

And, like all beloved and beauteous things
    She faded in distance and doubt away;
With only a tremble of snowy wings,
    She floated, swan-like, adown the bay,

Carrying with her a precious freight—

All I had gathered by years of pain;
A tempting prize to the pirate Fate,—
   And still I watch for her back again;

Watch for the earliest morning light,
   Till the pale stars grieve over the dying day,
To catch the gleam of her canvas white
   Among the islands which gem the bay,

But she comes not yet,—she will never come
   To gladden my eyes and my spirit more;
And my heart grows hopeless and faint and dumb
   As I wait and wait on the lonesome shore,

Knowing that tempest and time and storm
   Have wrecked and shattered my beauteous bark:
Rank sea-weeds cover her wasting form,
   And her sails are tattered and stained and dark.

But the tide comes up and the tide goes down,
   And the daylight follows the night's eclipse,
And till with the sailors, tanned and brown,
   I wait on the wharves and watch the ships.

And still, with a patience that is not hope,
   For vain and empty it long hath been,
I sit on the rough shore's rocky slope
   And watch to see if my ship comes in.

The Perplexed Housekeeper

Mrs. F. D. Gage

2 June 1871

I wish I had a dozen pair
    Of hands this very minute;
I'd soon put all these things to rights—
    The very deuce is in it.

Here's a big washing to be done,
    One pair of hands to do it—
Sheets, shirts and stockings, coats and pants—
    How will I e'er get through it?

Dinner to get for six or more,
    No loaf left o'er from Sunday,
And baby cross as he can live—
    He's always so on Monday.

And there's the cream, 'tis getting sour,
    And must forthwith be churning,
And here's Bob wants a button on—
    Which way shall I be turning?

'Tis time the meat was in the pot,
    The bread was worked for baking,
The clothes were taken from the boil—
    Oh dear! the baby's waking!

Oh dear! if P— comes home,
    And finds things in this bother,
He'll just begin and tell me all
    About his tidy mother.

How nice her kitchen used to be,

Her dinner always ready
Exactly when the dinner bell rung—
Hush, hush, dear little Freddy.

And then will come some hasty word,
    Right out before I'm thinking—
They say that hasty words from wives
    Set sober men to drinking.

Now isn't that a great idea,
    That men should take to sinning,
Because a weary, half-sick wife
    Can't always smile so winning?

When I was young I used to earn
    My living without trouble;
Had clothes and pocket money too,
    And hours of leisure double.

I never dreamed of such a fate,
    When I, a lass! was courted—
Wife, mother, nurse, seamstress, cook, housekeeper, chambermaid, laundress,   dairywoman and scrub generally doing the work of six
    For the sake of being supported.

Panning and Canning

Cold Turkey Substitute (and Stuffing)
Thomas Farringer-Logan

I.

Welcome's different than Bill had pictured: no homemade tempera-paint-and-butcher-paper-type banners, no marching band, no retired neighbors lining the suburban streets in lawn chairs waving, no cartwheeling newsies in patched jeans jogging alongside the truck shouting. "Top of the morning to you, Mr. Bill! Welcome back, Mr. Bentley!" No, none of that. Overhead, a passenger jet roars. People going somewhere Thanksgiving Day, Bill guesses, craning his neck inside Betsy, his truck of fourteen loyal years, as his hand on the door handle begins to shake.

"So I says, 'Listen, hon: Them delirium tremors can kill.' You hearing me, Bill? That's what I said," Smokey Dan yells and slams a hand down flat against the bar. "My lesser half wantin' to know why I don't up and quit my drinking, goddamn!"

II.

Bill's made it to the front door, her door, what was once their door--but he can't get white knuckles inches from the holiday wreath's autumn gourds to knock; both hands're shaking so badly. He breathes in deep. A man's gotta do what a man's—

Back outside Betsy, Bill's trembling hand can't fit the key in the lock before Karen calls out from the porch, stopping him cold. "Hello, William, we were beginning to wonder if you'd show."

Rows of goldenish bracelets clink as she crosses her arms, hugging herself against the cold. She's wearing a fine, flowy white dress thing. She looks good. Her hair's different. It's— Well, Bill doesn't really have the words to describe it right, but it looks good. It really does. He pictures himself in a tux in a ballroom with her and that hair—dancing under chandeliers. And, he must admit, too good for him. He reckons Karen might have just been being polite, inviting him when he ran into her at the grocery store last weekend and saw the turkey substitute in her cart and made some dumb joke.

"Bill!" she snaps, snapping him from his waltz. She's shaking her head. "Where you at?"

She recedes into the house. "I'm right here, Karen. I'm right here. With you," he whispers, shuffling across the frozen lawn.

Indoors, Karen's voice changes. Bill remembers it from when they used to, in her words, entertain company. He's that company now.

"Come in, come in. William Bentley, you remember Jesus, Dr. Jesus Cantu—"

"Please," Jesus interrupts. Bill follows the extended right hand from the J. of his J.C. cufflinks up along the light green medium-starch shirt, over the autumn-colored ascot and to the gaunt, mid-fifties cupid Mexican face he first met over a year ago. Bill grips the hollow, dissolving hand. Jesus says, "Call me Jim—or Jimmie if you'd prefer."

III.

Bill adjusts his belt buckle, then releases the big front bumper; tries finding some other place for his hands before settling on dangling interlaced fingers like a hammock for his gut. For lack of better words and better than to be thought a fool, he says nothing. Unlike the warm silences of the bar, this silence is uncomfortable. Opposite him, equally quiet, Karen. And on her either side, the Chris-es.

(Soft focus as Karen's bookends tilt their dirty blond heads away from their mom in a manner endearing to our regular TV viewers and a melody from an unplaceable sitcom flutes in light jazz beats in the back of Bill's head.) The younger, Kris with a "k," short for Kristopherson, Karen's surprise after the ink dried on her second divorce, nearabouts when, briefly living on her own and working as a waitress at The Skillet, she met William (Bill) Bentley – Kris diagnosed ADHD last year and has more recently discovered that cats don't always land on their feet when dropped from a roof in a plastic shopping bag (canned audience gasps) – and Christina, Kris's older sister born shortly after Karen's marriage ended to her high school sweetheart Christian Oliver, one of two hundred and ninety-three U.S. servicemen to die in Desert Storm, she – precociously after only fifteen years on this Earth – has determined that all men are jackasses (abundant audience applause) and reads at the college level. Karen's quiet.

Jesus returns from hanging Bill's coat in the hall closet and side-hugs Karen and smiles. Additional silence. The standing grandfather clock, which the retirement home forbade, and so her semi-senile, former military sergeant father bequeathed her and Bill to commemorate their one-year anniversary, chimes and Bill is officially half an hour late.

Wind the clock back to yesterday afternoon. Capture Bill's eyes opening then slowly pan clockwise from the living room couch across the prefab's wall of televisions (one for sound, one for the picture, and one – bad A. and V., people all green and sound like they're talking on CBs – for watching another channel during commercials atop an entirely broken RCA there for support and symmetry; their HD TV's at the bar), past peeling pistachio cabinets he'll get around to stripping and painting one of these days when he's a blessed moment to breathe or a wild hair up his ass, and up to Ma cooking on the electric skillet on the stove who says, "You didn't have to say yes. She was just being polite."

"I know, Ma, I know. It's just lunch."

Ma, still in her houseslippers and showercap frying up Bill's early afternoon eggs, is probably still upset about him taking off, her having to run the whole shebang – tomorrow's annual barbeque bird day at Lars' Bar as busy as the bar'll get 'til Christmas – by her lonesome, selling ice-cold six packs at eight-fifty a pop and she's getting up there in years.

"Do you? She's not coming back, William."

Bill wishes the camera were on him so he could see his reaction. He hadn't, until Ma just said, considered the possibility of winning Karen back. Not really.

"You're a smart boy, son – you scored in the top twentieth percentile on your Postal 470 Exam, for Pete's sake – can't you see? She's a no-good money-grubber. She's happy now where she is, with that beaner doctor bringing home the bacon, the chorizo. Now eat your eggs and be quiet."

Time's slowed, and everyone's quiet still and fake-smiling like some hidden photographer's having equipment problems. Bill's stomach burns. Might be an ulcer. Could be cancer. The room is kinda blurry when he hears himself say, "Where's the pis—I do mean, 'wash room' in this here fine abode, madam?"

"Where it's always been, Bill."

"Hope I don't get lost," says our Bill Bentley and chuckles to himself because no one else finds him funny.

The house: It stayed in her name; it has not stayed the same. Where they'd been saving to put furniture in the front room, Bill now passes the formal oak dining table she always wanted surrounded by six matching high-backed chairs. All those years she read all them magazines and watched all them programs on TV, it's like walking into her private dream room— flat silk floral arrangement on the wall, porcelain angel collection filling the curio, her and Jesus' personalized Wiccan wedding vows in a glass case—

but none of it looks real or lasting. Like those half-books and TVs made of cardboard in department store showrooms, it's just for show and looks to Bill like he might still have a chance.

IV.

"Another of the same, barkeep, and let's keep'em coming."

Bill washes his hands in the kids' bathroom sink, scrubbing hard and getting under the cuticles where germs like to hide. It was in this room one night not too long ago, not really, back when it was still their house and this their guest bath, he'd locked the door and refused to leave. He's so much better now, he really is, but at the time his bones ached, felt brittle, threatened to snap at the joints like cricket legs. He was curled up in a ball that night because he couldn't get up and into the tub. Though he knew the warm water would help ease the flow of blood out his forearms. Those animated squiggly germs from that tile cleaner commercial were in his mind, and he just couldn't, just couldn't anything anymore back then.

"What's your poison, partner?"

The kids, it was the middle of the night, they were in their beds safe asleep, but Karen, she heard him sobbing, must've wondered why he was in there. She said, "It's okay, Bill. It's okay. Just unlock the door, let me in." Then putting her arms around him, his tears wetting her nightgown, his face buried in her bosom, her one hand rubbing the back of his head, the other helping squeeze a towel staunching the flow of blood, and she didn't scream or yell like he feared she would or wake up the kids. She said calmly and kept saying, "It's okay. It's all okay." It must have been downright embarrassing, holding her husband, a grown man – naked, sobbing, bleeding, unemployed – as she rocked him in her arms. To spare her further trouble, Bill left the very next day. Or at least that's what he likes to say.

"Closing time, folks. You ain't gotta go home, but you can't stay here."

Bill, by force of will first unballing his fists, splashes some water on his face. His mirror self, making a determined face, a fighter's mug, catches Bill staring. Alright, champ, now's your chance. Get in that ring and pull no polite-guy, good-father punches. Hit'em with the poor-me combo if ya gotta. Just get out there, slugger, & clean that no-good carpetbagger's clock already. Ding-ding-ding.

V.

Bill finds his place. There are two unlit candles in two silver candlestick holders, five plates, five bowls, five fluted water glasses with water no ice, five wine glasses filled with chilled sparkling organic cider, five napkins in five pewter napkin rings, five knives, ten spoons, and ten forks on the table. The china is from The Republic of Formosa, a wedding gift from her second marriage, and the silver is real. Every piece in its proper place. Kris sits dwarfed in his high-backed chair beside Bill who sits next to Jesus who sits next to Karen who sits next to Christina who sits across from her new father, Kris sits across from his mother, and Bill sits across from an empty seat. Kris pauses his portable videogame and takes hold of Bill's hand. Bill bows his head; the family lifts theirs toward the ceiling. Jesus begins.

"We gather to give thanks for this, Your bounty, on this, Your day, a blessing symbolizing the communion of all peoples of the Earth, all races, creeds, and ethnicities. Glorious Powers Above, grant those gathered around Your table to partake of this bounty Gaia has provided that we, your humble children, may be of open minds and not criticize neighbors until we have first walked a mile in their moccasins. And may we," pause for his children and wife to join in, which, despite what sounds to Bill's ears like cult-like creepiness, they do, "observe the sanctity of all life on this great planet, our only one, and appreciate our differences with kindness and love and respect for all so to honor and reveal the All That is One. This is our prayer. Amen."

Game unpauses, Christina takes gum from her mouth, and Bill the lapsed Baptist stares dumbfounded, thinking, That was different.

"Those were some fine words there, Jimmie. And here I thought you all were all black cats and love potion number nines."

Jesus smiles and begins to explain something in his serious-casual manner. Bill expresses awkwardness through a gesture he's seen on TV, but they are only confused. He goes back to pushing his polite portion of Tofurkey around under the cover of lumpy veggie gravy before putting a large – almost too large – forkful of potatoes and mashed turkey substitute into his mouth.

VI.

Subjects of their (eventual) conversation: everyone's job ("And that would allow us to marry, pardon the pun, the therapeutic practice, that is, my marriage counseling, with our developing spiritual understanding." "Hunh, you don't say." "Indeed I do, Bill." "Well, Jimmie, I've been making up some plans of my own. You know, maybe figuring on expanding out the bar." "So Lars' Bar is doing well. Attracting new clientele?" "Some," a lie. "And it sounds like you're taking charge," Karen. "Some," another. "You're happy at the bar?" Jesus. "Sure. What other job besides Congressman or airplane pilot lets you drink at work? Just joshing." "You don't (hand gesture) then when you're working?" "At all?" Karen adds. "Oh, I— Some."), what the kids are doing in school (Bill, searching, "So, uh, how they doing in school, the kids?" Jesus proud, "Bill, you really helped rear two astute scholars, which I suppose you already knew, but, still, you have every right to be proud. Stupendous students. Christina reads at the college level."), what was on TV last night ("Actually, Bill, we don't watch much television around here."), local politics ("Thumbs up their asses." "Well, it appears we have a difference of opinion on this particular issue, Bill, but we are all entitled to, and should respect, our differences."), the weather ("Sure could've used some more of that rain before it froze." "We do rain dances," Kris offers, looking up from his game to take a second forkful of stuffing, his third bite all meal. "Occasionally," Karen qualifies. Jesus explains, "It's more a social-slash-spiritual cognition repatterning than an actual alteration of meteorological precipitation. Have you ever the opportunity to read any Carlos Castaneda, Bill?" "The baseball player?"), and so on until the safer subjects exhausted.

Teeth on teeth and silverware scraping against plates, eyes avert, wondering quietly what else there is to say. A chair creaks as Bill shifts his weight. This quiet is not his ally.

Bill Bentley needs an edge. History, memories are his edge. Lovers' intimacy, life as man and wife. Bill wonders if Jesus knows that Karen was molested by her uncle. Wonders if he knows a whole slew of things about her, which he probably does; he's a counselor after all. Still, there's gotta be something he—

"Rascal's dead. Yee—up, buried him last month. Someone hit'em, drove right on off. Nobody got a good look at the plates or nothing. Rascal, he… Well, he didn't make it."

Karen, "What?"

"Yee-up. Sure was a good dog, that Rascal. Didn't know how to sit or roll over or nothing like that, but, still, dog like that, that's still a good dog. An ordinary dog, you know. Real loyal. And that's just what some people need. Loyalty."

"You didn't call?"

A phone rings. Coincidence appreciated by all. Kris pauses his game, registers reactions, and returns to killing bad guys.

"I should take this."

"Woh, fourteen and a CEO already, Christy?" Bill joshes. "Got any hot stock tips for your old old man?"

But they're not laughing. It's a tough crowd, and they don't see the humor.

"Rascal died?"

"I'm fifteen. And it's my phone, Bill," calling him by his first name and relishing it. "I pay all my bills. Yez, what'p, Lisa? Yeah, I know. Totally. Fo' rilly? Me too. L-O-L. Totes. Like I'm eating dinner too! Yeah, I'm all over that shizzel fo' realzel."

"That's what she needs a phone for?"

"Rascal died?"

"Do you mind? I'm on the phone."

"Takes after her mother."

No laughs.

VII.

"Rascal died?"

"Rascal died, Karen."

Jesus, "Would you take the conversation to the other room, honey?"

Christina leaves. Everyone's serious and quiet again. Bill shouldn't have come; he's not feeling well. Meanwhile, Kris, tongue in the corner of his mouth, advances to the next level.

"This is supposed to be a holiday period of peace, Bill," Karen says, simmering but, Bill can see, still trying to work herself back up to a boil.

"Actually-" Jesus tries.

"And how could you, after all these— I mean, Rascal. Rascal wasn't just yours, you know. You didn't even call? You didn't even bother saying anything in the store? No. You didn't. Not a word. And then you go avoid the subject by yelling at Christina-"

"Did I yell? Did I yell?"

"No, Bill, you didn't 'yell,' but, you know, this is stupid. This is supposed to be a peaceful, a, uh, peaceful period of holiday celebration."

"Actually," Jesus' flatware – a knife and fork he eats in tandem with – return to their original place settings as he sits straighter in his chair, a posture he assumes when pontificating, "the first Thanksgiving was extremely violent. The Native American tribe of Wamapanoag utterly refused to pray to the White man's god, and the Puritans – intolerant of alternative cultures they had prejudged 'primitive' – it was quite literally all these religious fundamentalists could do to abstain from violence. Thanksgiving, contrary to popular conception and the necessities of myth, was not a pleasant affair."

"Well, I'm sure all their hootin' and hollarin' and dancin' around must've bothered 'em. Woo-woo-woo-woo," Bill, hand beating against mouth, mimics the high-pitched, childhood sounds of John Wayne versus the Injuns. "Wo-" Christ.

No laughter, much appalled disbelief, which Christina must sense from the other room because she capers back in for front row seats.

"So that was uncomfortable," Jesus, bringer of peace, says when the color returns to his paled face. He straightens in his chair. "You know, Bill..."

VIII.
What Bill wouldn't give for a shot of Jack and a cold one right about now. How he'd survived a half decade-and-change of marriage without a drop he'll never understand. Bill breaks his bread and cleans cranberry sauce off his plate, trying to ignore Karen and Jesus' tensed faces and mouthed words. They're talking about him. Everyone's talking about him. Let'em talk. Bill doesn't care.

"I wish I was a cow," Ed the Head said, sitting on the other end of the Chevy's tailgate after-hours with Bill as the morning sun came up and the dew grew on the lawn. Ed had just been diagnosed with the Big C, only villain ornery enough to stop John Wayne. "You see how much grass there is out there, Bill? I'd probably need an extra two stomachs, but hey, still, no problems, guy, no problems. Live outta the van just eating grass. Happiness is eating grass. Surely."

"So?"

Karen somehow manages to speak volumes with that one word, a concise compendium of Bill's every wrong.

"So?" she demands.

Then starts crying.

"Oh, there, there. Come here, Kare Bear," Jesus, patting his shoulder, says to Karen acting crazy. Her husband closes his eyes and slowly strokes her sobbing head. Meanwhile, a distant clinking sound like a railroad crossing grows louder and faster.

It's Bill's hand rattling his fork against his plate. The shakes are back. And the headache. Brain tumor? All day long he's had this headache. Allergies, a lot of pollen, phlegm, drainage, back of his throat itchy since this morning when he woke up early. Would explain his problems keeping attention lately. He had a cyst on his ear; a cyst is a type of tumor, and tumors spread...

Would they call, though, that's the question. Would they call the ambulance or just watch as William Charles Bentley died here on their lacy tablecloth when a sudden aneurysm leaves his paralytic face drooling frozen wide-eyed? Would they keep on eating their tasteless lunch off their fancy china plates as if nothing had happened? Would they let him rot, step over him every day on the way to work and school like he never even existed?

IX.

A cigarette finally lit, Bill paces. He'd – hot in the hoof – made some excuse and then out to his truck but then recalled the keys are in his coat back in the house so now he paces along the garden between Karen's and the neighbor's house. He planted this, the gladiolas, the rosebush, the cherry tomatoes, broke and turned the soil with a rented tiller, sowed the seeds, spread the fertilizer, and now it's bearing fruit. Seven years hence. He used to come home and kiss the Chris-es' little heads in their sleep. Kristopher was just a baby. Guess no one ever saw that, though. He'll have to take this secret goodness with him to the grave.

"Ya know, Bill, you're a stand-up, real-good guy. You never let your momma down, and you're good at cards. Just keep it up is all. Look deep inside yourself, you'll see what I mean," Ed the Head had said, his handyman's tanned, epidermal leather against the white of bedsheets. Hospital antiseptic couldn't cover the stench of stale piss and poop. Ed coughed death, and Bill winced, knowing it wouldn't be long. Two days later, no one mentioned anything at the bar, just a round on the house when the call came.

A gentle wind blows through the subdivision. Bill sees most of the leaves have fallen from the trees. A guy jogger jogs by with two percent body fat followed by a younger, female version, a recent mom behind an aerodynamic stroller. In the distance, children released from holiday captivity howl. Bill watches his breath in the late-November air, then a very male squirrel, testicles kissing the ground as it darts across the asphalt, sprints along on the tips of its toes, and for a brief moment, the fullness and limits of life, nay, LIFE ITSELF is bare before Bill and he sees: Only thing you've got to do in this life is live, keep yourself fed and roof over your head.

But life lurks. Bill knows. Bill's fully aware. It waits for you to make a mistake. He hasn't had medical insurance since he worked for the Post Office. Body's just like a car, starts to break down after a while; mortal existence complicated that way. And can't control everything, not even part of the time. You know this planet's just a spinning mass of rock in the middle of empty space? We're just a small speck in the universe. And then there's Karen. Karen and the kids in the mornings when he can't get to sleep, Karen and the kids in the afternoons when he wakes up, when he brushes his teeth, when he mows the narrow patches of dying grass and weeds outside Ma's house.

Bill feels like crying but has forgotten how. And here is Dr. Jesus Cantu politely smiling and holding Bill's coat out to him.

"Hi, Bill. Am I interrupting? Let me know if this is an unwelcomed inquiry, but what are you doing out here in the cold, friend?"

"Just smoking a cigarette, Jim. Nothing really." Bill's voice unsteady, chattering with cold and nerves, as it sometimes gets around these head-shrink types who – experience shows – can twist your words all around and make you say anything by the time they get done. Seeing as they always knew what they wanted you to say, Bill never understood why they – a he then a she then another he then no more job and no more therapy – couldn't just slip him a crib sheet and save them both the time and trouble of hearing what they needed to hear so they could go on and prescribe the pills they were going to give him anyway. "Just a cigarette."

"'Sometimes a cigar is only a cigar.'"

Bill, defensive, taking his coat back, avers, "Just a cigarette."

"It's Freud." Weirdness prevails. Jesus sighs. "Sigmund Freud? Never mind. So, you—"

"No, of course, the psychiatry guy. So you come out, Jim, and bring me my coat in a polite means of telling me to get?"

"Well, actually, Bill, I was hoping I could solicit your assistance in stringing up some Solstice lights. Hey," Jesus' touch has Bill jump and Bill accidentally meets Jesus' sparkling pair peering from the depths of a face jelly-like with concern. "I'm glad you came. You made the right choice. Besides, I believe a little conflict strengthens family by allowing contrary forces to comingle. Without oppositionals, you can't create a current of dialogue needed to spark the life flows that recharge the life battery.

"So, Bill, in short, to answer your initial question: No, I don't desire you to leave. I believe your presence means more to the Chris-es than the kids can comfortably express in front of their mom and new dad. But what I'd really like—honestly, Bill—is if we could work together not to upset Karen anymore today. How about it, huh?"

Bill shrugs, but Jesus is already cheerily leading the way.

X.
Int. Garage/Rec Room.

"Like what you did with the garage, Jim," Bill shouts, accepting the fourteen-foot aluminum extension ladder over the like-new poker and foosball tables. Bill's tools and spare parts and projects-in-progress sold in a garage sale before the divorce was final. "Looks real tidy."

XI.

A car passes. Jesus smiles and waves. "Thanks, Bill. So, if you're fine here, I'll go retrieve the lights."

Bill raises the ladder under the overhang near a dead hornet nest and remembers what it was like having a wife, that even watching TV was better with someone else around. That's not quite right. Not just any someone.

Start up the projector, dim the lights. "Memories of Karen, Reel One." Here she is in the morning, face still a little puffy and wearing that robe she always wore, putting a second ketchup and bologna sandwich and extra vitamins in his sack lunch. Oh, and here she is late at night wearing those librarian reading glasses as she takes care of the bills, always on top of matters like how to spend the money and where the kids need to be at and at what time and what should go where in the cabinets and on the counters and around the house and why Bill needed a new belt so his leathers would match so he'd get that promotion. And here she is, brunette hair with gold highlights and with her fancy nails she'd splurge on, treating herself just a bit once a month, but in this shifting memory's moments her hair's pinned close to her scalp and she's rolling up her stockings to go to that part-time job she had there for a couple of months before one night coming home from an office party and she didn't want to talk about it, her hair being all out of place, and asked him pretty pretty pretty please no more questions and gave him that pout and said that maybe he should seek counseling after all because she just can't live like this with a husband always sick.

Bill sees the ascended figure of Jesus on the ladder above him, the sweater still draped over his shoulders, a string of lights in one hand. What a dweeb. Bill can't imagine this feller in bed with Karen, giving it to her the way Bill used to, real hard, real mean sometimes too.

The sun stabs at his blinking eyes, giving Jesus a nimbus of winter light as Bill below recognizes the ladder is only a slender contraption made of aluminum and feels the wind shift, bringing with it the scented smells of the garden. And so it goes, the heave and pitch of the Earth. It moves too fast. Bill grips the ladder tight, but it's too late.

XII.

Long moments as Jesus struggles to his knees and manages his feet. Karen's fourth-and-present lesser-half stumbles in reverse, backing away from the scene in a crouch, cut palms open before him wanting no trouble.

"He…" Jesus says and says no more, unable to explain to Karen who's sprinted from the doorway to touch the wounds on her husband's hands in disbelief. She clutches him close to her chest, staring viciously at Bill, putting herself between them. Though she wasn't there, didn't see, Bill wants to say and help but can't.

"Talk to me. Are you okay? Say something. What's my maiden name? Is there anything you can't remember? Anything broken?"

"I… Bill…"

Bill Bentley trails behind, back into their house. Children emerge from their rooms, a videogame on pause, plans for the mall put on hold. It's the DTs, Bill tells himself, studying his hands white and shaking. His face contorts in a variety of apologetic expressions.

"I didn't— I mean, Karen, Jimmie, I-I thought, but I didn't mean… Or was ever really actually gonna-"

Bill feels his body's weight on its bones, the nerves in his scalp, the cooling sweat on his brow. They'll be beautiful again once he leaves. It'll all be back to normal tomorrow. Bill will return to being a distant memory no one talks about once he walks out that door, forgotten except on the rare Thanksgiving when one of them might kinda-sorta remember him and what happened today but not feel it worth the mentioning.

"I'm sorry," Bill apologizes, not just for the accident but for everything. There is silence in the room. From the kitchen, the sound of water spilling onto the linoleum from an overflowing sink followed by the discordant clang as the grandfather clock striking half-past is smashed by a high-backed chair before Bill leaves with Betsy, peeling out through the garden, not to be forgotten.

Angels of the Drunk
Tim Pfau

We lay there flat, supine at the juncture,
the center point, where Commercial and Court
cross at 2:20 AM undisturbed,
by autos or other passing strangers.
Eight blocks away, a freight train clanged and howled
but closing-time traffic rumbled elsewhere,
perhaps closer to Motel 6's beds.
Bands were done playing. The good people slept.
Overcome, we sought rest between our sins,
pedestrian lapses, rum's transgressions,
heedless breaches of faith and compassion.
Only luck kept us from falling asleep,
luck of the draw, tarred angels of the drunk.

Me and the Trees

Allyson Myers

the Apple trees Listen to Mommy
she Whispers to Me and the Trees how
her Dreams all came True cause of Me and
the Trees and she Hugs me and Kisses
me Hands me a Dandy and Tells me
to Make up a Wish and to Blow so
that All of the Hairs will go Flying
like Me in my Tutu the Grasses
they Reach for my Skirt and the Trees smile
down On me like Dad from the House where
he Brings home the Bacon like Mom all
ways Tells him he Waves through the Window
and Blows to me Kisses and Turns back to Work so
i Turn to the Trees and they Reach their
long Branches so High in the Sky i
can't Reach so in Stead i lie Down in
the Grass looking Up i can See the
blades Stretch to the Sun and the Sky is
a Canvas on Which trees are Painted
and Thoughts on their Branches grow Pink and
stay Green and die Yellow like Dandies.

Peaches

Lois Rosen

You're not gonna waste a crop like that,
not with what they charge at the IGA
and factory-canned never tastes flavourful
not after you've enjoyed home-canned.
Pick Fairhavens and Elbertas.
They grow best in this valley.
In the hot, then cold
makes 'em easier to peel.
Feed the peel to the cattle.
They love the snack.
Sometimes I even think I taste
a hint of that sweetness
in the meat.
Let the fruit cool good
and use a real sharp knife
to slice them even.
Quarters pack easier than halves.
Pour in syrup,
tighten the lids,
but not too much,
and be sure to time the boil.
What I love best
is how the kitchen smells, fragrant.
Make sure all the screens
on the windows are shut tight
or the butterflies and bees
flit in here to sip the pools
of juice on the counter.
Who can blame them?
The hardest part is lifting
the huge kettle off the stove.

There's no one to call for help
when crops need harvesting

and the men are on the combine
sunup to sundown.
No, I don't can every last peach.
A good batch, a couple of bushels worth,
I cut up raw, sprinkle with preservative
and put in freezer bags for baking.
You tell me now what beats
homemade peach pie, cobbler,
or waffles topped with dollops of fresh cream,
and I'll tell you nothing in this world tastes better.

BSM30
Brandon McMullen

The road less traveled
is not for me, just look at
The Donner Party

Those Who Can't
David Jordan

It was Doug Cooper's first teaching job.

The ink barely dry on his new master's degree, he had been a last-minute hire, benefiting from a long-standing friendship with the recently selected chairman of the Journalism Department. Doug arrived in Guthrie, Iowa, home of Hoover State College, with his wife, Tess, and daughter, Liza, after a four-day drive from Eugene, Oregon, in mid-August, a scant three days before classes began.

He scrambled desperately to assemble lesson plans, order textbooks, generate syllabi. Through the first week of the semester, he ripped the final pages of his lectures from his office typewriter as the bell rang and sprinted the length of the building to deliver them to sweaty, sleepy students. The temperature soared past a hundred degrees each afternoon on the Iowa flatlands, and weary classroom air-conditioners groaned and whistled but did little to alleviate the heat.

Doug greeted the weekend with relief. He planned to spend his time away from the campus preparing lectures, in hopes of becoming more coherent in class. There had been instances when he realized, after spinning from typewriter to classroom and back to the office, he couldn't remember anything he had said in the last hour and a half. He felt blurred, out of control.

He had been hired as an instructor, a temporary, one-year fill-in for an assistant professor who bolted on short notice to take a big-money job as public relations director for a Des Moines electronics company. A department search committee would use the next year to select a tenure-track replacement. If Doug wanted the permanent job, and he did, he needed to impress with his interim performance. He had to gain a grip on his work.

Friday night, laboring in the spare bedroom of his rented house six blocks north of the campus, he put together a solid lecture for his Monday morning Intro class. It took him until after midnight. Finally he crawled into bed with Tess, slid an arm around her warm waist, and fell asleep with visions of a gigantic pile of textbooks toppling toward him. He arose before seven, paused only long enough to make coffee, and returned to his books and typewriter to work on his lecture for the Monday afternoon Reporting I class. He was dismayed when the kitchen phone rang at nine o'clock and Tess, after answering, came to say Beverly Nichols had invited them to dinner that evening. He wanted to stay home, to continue working on his lectures. He had to get ahead, avoid bombarding students with gibberish.

"But you should make friends with other people on the faculty, shouldn't you?" Tess asked. "Isn't that part of the departmental politics thing?"

"I suppose." Doug sighed. He had spoken with Beverly Nichols in the hallways two or three times, but never for more than a moment.

"Joe Luzinski will be there with his wife, too. He has the office next to yours, right?"

Doug nodded. "Tell her we'll come. Do we have to find a sitter?"

"No, she said to bring Liza. She can wear her new dress."

Liza had begun first grade in the elementary school up the hill. The new dress, green velvet with a white lace collar, was a consolation prize her mother had bought her to soothe the pain of moving to Iowa and leaving behind her neighborhood school in Oregon. Neither Liza nor Tess were particularly pleased to find themselves, all of a sudden, two thousand miles from the comforts of extended family, familiar places, customary routines. The Hoover State job was a career opportunity he couldn't pass up, Doug kept telling Tess, and himself.

They reached Beverly Nichols' house at 6:30. She met them at the door, brandishing a highball glass and a grin. The Luzinskis sat on a sofa in the parlor. Introductions flowed.

Joe Luzinski was a boxy man, with a square-cornered crewcut, pock-marked face, thick shoulders. He taught broadcasting. He had learned radio broadcasting in the Army, right out of high school, then had gone to college on the G.I. Bill. He'd done the course work for his Ph.D. at a college in Ohio, but hadn't finished writing his dissertation. He had been hired three years earlier with the understanding he would complete the dissertation while teaching. He was due for a tenure decision in the spring. If the dissertation, dusty pages of which lay in teetering stacks on tables, file cabinets and window sills in his office, were not completed by spring, he would be denied tenure and, in effect, fired. The department head, Derek Cahill, had told Doug all this while delivering thumbnail sketches of the faculty the day he arrived on campus.

Luzinski's wife, Debby, undoubtedly had been gorgeous at twenty but now—fifteen years later—appeared over-ripe, with a small double chin, a sagging jawline, a slight pot belly beneath her stylish gray gabardine skirt. Her hair remained glistening black and tumbled to the middle of her back. Her eyes were a gaudy violet, accentuated by dramatic makeup, and she wore bright red lipstick.

The hostess, Beverly Nichols, was a tall, sturdy woman of forty or so with short-cropped blond hair, a long, horsy face and thick eyeglasses. She wore a yellow cotton dress with a skirt supported by crinoline that made it flounce around her knees.

"What can I get you to drink?" she asked as the Coopers settled into armchairs, Liza on her mother's lap. "We're having gin and tonic." She gestured at the Luzinskis. "It's so damn hot. Only mad dogs and Englishmen go out in the Iowa sun, and then they cool off with gin and tonic."

"Gin and tonic would be fine," said Doug.

Tess shook her head. "I don't need anything, thanks."

"White wine? I've got red, too. Or a beer?"

"No, no. I'm fine."

"Pepsi? Pepsi for the little one? What's your name again, honey? My Erica is around somewhere. You two need to play."

Liza repeated her name, agreed to accept a Pepsi. Beverly strode out of the room, swishing in her crinoline.

Debby Luzinski smiled. "You folks are from Oregon. We're not from around here, either. We came from Pittsburgh."

"Nobody comes from around here but the students," said Luzinski. "Bev is from Illinois. Katie Graves came from Alabama. Curt Mooney started out in Texas. It's the old academic merry-go-round."

"I thought you were from Ohio," Doug told Luzinski.

"I went to grad school there. I grew up in Pittsburgh. I met Debby in Pittsburgh."

"I had a TV show in Pittsburgh!" Debby grinned. "A talk show, five mornings a week. I interviewed Stephen King, Frank Borman, Goldie Hawn."

Her husband nodded, smiled. "She was a star."

"Well, I was!" Debby shot Joe a look of reproach, feigned or real. "I gave up stardom to marry a professor." She laughed.

Joe's smile disappeared. He looked at Doug, and then at the floor.

"This is Erica." Beverly Nichols pushed a girl of about ten through the kitchen doorway. She was tall and skinny, with lank blonde hair. "Why don't you and -- Liza, is it? -- go check out the Barbie dolls in your bedroom?"

Erica stalked through the parlor. She glanced back at Liza as she disappeared into a hallway. Tess pushed her daughter off her lap and gestured for her to follow. Reluctantly, she did.

Beverly returned from the kitchen with two fresh gin and tonics. She handed one to Doug, sipped the other. "Drink up. I'm two or three ahead of you. It's so damn hot!"

She sank with a flourish onto a loveseat in front of the picture window, her skirt flaring and rustling. "So! Tell me about yourself. What's in Oregon, besides cowboys and Indians?"

"Lots of rain," Doug answered. "Actually, a lot more rain than cowboys. Or Indians. The west isn't as wild as it used to be."

"Larry Mahan was on my show once," Debby inserted. "You know Larry Mahan? He was in town with the rodeo."

Everyone nodded, smiled, even those who had never heard of him.

"I understand you and Derek Cahill went to college together," Beverly said, "As undergrads. In Oregon."

"He was two years ahead of me. Recruited me to write for the campus paper when he was managing editor."

"And now he's fetched you all the way to Iowa."

"I like Derek," said Debby. "He's nice."

Beverly glanced at Debby. "I don't know about nice, but he's smart. Talented. A good man."

Derek Cahill was six-foot-two and weighed two hundred and sixty pounds. When he and the five-seven, one hundred and forty-pound Doug walked together, Tess had once said, they looked like a St. Bernard and a Chihuahua sauntering along.

"Beverly was runner-up when Derek was elected department chairman," said Luzinski. "They split the votes. It was close."

"I won't ask who you voted for, Joe." Beverly laughed, took a swallow of her gin and tonic. "But I suspect you went for Derek. He doesn't have his doctorate, either."

Luzinski winced, but managed a smile. "Beverly is Doctor Nichols, of course. From Southern Illinois University. In Carbondale, right?"

"Right. A degree mill if ever there was one, but I got my union card. I pity you poor bastards."

"I'll be done by spring," Luzinski assured her.

"I suppose, and within two years Derek Cahill will leave us to chase his. Can't last long without that union card."

Doug, owner of a mere master's degree himself, looked at Luzinski, shrugged. Luzinski shrugged back.

"So they've got you teaching skills courses, I suppose," Beverly said to Doug. "A million papers to grade. You really do need to get your doctorate, union card or no, so you can teach theory courses. They're much easier. I specialize in communications theory, and a little law. I handle one skills class a semester, usually copy editing, just to do my bit. I sure as hell wouldn't specialize in them."

Luzinski shifted in his seat. "I teach skills courses. Broadcast newswriting, stuff like that. They're no big deal."

"Yes, but how well do you teach them, Professor Luzinski?" Beverly lifted her drink. "You know what they say -- those who can, do. Those who can't, teach."

Luzinski winced again, this time without a smile. Beverly grinned and waved a dismissive hand at him. "Just a joke. You do a fine job. We all do a fine job. Teaching is a calling, you know. Like preaching."

Her daughter appeared in the doorway. "Can we have some soda? Can we take some Pepsi to my room?"

"Oh, shoot!" Beverly bounced to her feet. "I was going to give Lisa -- Lisa? Liza -- some Pepsi, and I forgot." She bustled out of the room, followed by Erica.

When they returned, the girl carried a can of Pepsi Cola in each hand. Beverly swatted her fanny as she walked away. "Erica! Looks like me, don't you think? Named after her dad, that cretin, but she looks just like I did at that age."

Beverly returned to the loveseat. "I'm divorced, you knew that. Eric lives in Peoria. Erica hasn't seen him for sixteen months. The shitheel." She gulped more gin and tonic.

"Ann Landers came on the show once," Debby Luzinski said. "She talked about divorce. She said it was like an epidemic in this country."

Beverly eyed Debby. "How long have you been married?"

"Three years. The wedding was just before we came to Iowa."

"No kids."

"No, but we have the world's nicest cat. Chekky. Short for Chekhov."

Luzinski shook his head. "That cat is so fat his belly drags the floor when he walks. I've never seen anything like it."

"I got him right after we moved here," Debby said. "It took some adjustment. One day, you're on television with Ann Landers, and the next you're alone in the middle of Iowa while your husband spends all his time teaching. Chekky became my companion. He's my pal. My kindred spirit. Mi amigo."

"He's going to die of blocked plumbing if he doesn't get rid of some of that weight."

"No, he's not! Don't say that! There's nothing wrong with his -- his -- plumbing, or whatever." Debby took a large swallow from her gin and tonic.

Luzinski gazed at his wife, blinking. "Sorry."

"Well, don't say mean things about Chekky."

"Neither of you was married before?" Beverly asked.

"What?" Debby swung her violet eyes to her hostess. "Oh, no. Joe is my first. And I'm his. First, last and always." She giggled.

"Three years ago? You both had to be in your thirties. Weren't you a bit long of tooth for a first marriage?"

Debby drew up straight in her chair. "I was thirty-one, if it matters. And it doesn't."

"I was thirty-three," Joe added.

Beverly drained her glass. "Maybe that's the secret to not divorcing. Marry late. Ask Ann Landers about it next time you see her."

"Joe and I are very happy," Debby replied. "Aren't we, baby?"

Joe smirked. "Yes, ma'am."

"That sounded sincere." Debby cocked an eyebrow at him. "That sounded about sincere and a half."

Luzinski shrugged. "We're a lot happier than people thought we'd be."

Debby laughed loudly, fixed Doug and Tess with a sardonic stare. "We had a dramatic wedding."

"Meaning?" inquired Beverly.

Debby laughed again, looked to her husband. "You tell it."

"Well," Joe said, "it happened kind of quick. I'd finished my doctoral course work in June, and I'd been hired to come out here in August, so I went back to Pittsburgh to visit family, see some old friends. One night in July, right before the fourth, I went to a party. One of my old radio buddies, a guy I worked with at a station in Harrisburg, was throwing it. Debby was there, and we met."

"He was star-struck," Debby interjected.

Joe nodded. "True. Here was this beautiful woman. I'd seen her on TV, of course. But in person, she was even more beautiful."

"Flatterer." Debby pretended to primp her hair with a hand.

"I talked with her for a long time. She seemed sort of -- what? unhappy? It struck me as odd a woman so good-looking could feel so bad about things."

"I'd been having health problems," Debby said.

"So I tried to cheer her up."

"He made me laugh."

"I told her jokes. And I asked her out."

"And three weeks later, we got married!" Debby said. "And the next day, we left for Iowa."

"Quick and painless," observed Doug.

"It was a little more complicated than that," Luzinski said.

"It must have been." Beverly rose from the loveseat to fetch another round of gin and tonics. "Beautiful TV star marries ugly old Joe Luzinski? Who'd believe it?" She laughed, then added as she walked from the room: "Just kidding, Joe. You know I think you're a doll."

"Yeah, right." Joe rolled his eyes. "No, I realize it looks like a mismatch. I look like King Kong, and she looks like -- well, like Debby McKay."

"That was my maiden name," said Debby. "McKay. Actually, it was McKillop, but I changed it. McKillop is so clunky. I wasn't just on TV, you know. I started out to be an actress. I was in New York for three years before I went back to Pittsburgh and did television. I always figured McKay would look better on a theater marquee. It's easier to say, too. I did theater things in Pittsburgh, even when I was on television. I was in 'A Doll's House.' Did you ever see that? Ibsen. My reviews were quite good. But I got on TV as a weather girl -- reading the forecasts, you know? And then I went on the talk show. And the money was so much better than I could make in theater, I sort of drifted away from it."

"But you were willing to quit television and get married and move to Iowa after knowing Joe only three weeks?" Tess asked.

"Her show got canned," Joe said.

"It did not!" Debby said. "The show stayed on. They just decided they wanted somebody different to co-host. I was the co-host, you know, and they kept Mike Mann, but they wanted a different type to work with him. Somebody blonde and cutesy, I guess."

"Somebody younger," Joe murmured.

Debby knifed him with a glare, turned to Doug and Tess with a brave smile. "I was replaced by a twenty-two-year-old slut, the producer's girl-friend. She jumped from the University of Pittsburgh to his bed, and from his bed to my show."

Beverly returned to the room, distributed more drinks. "Not a lot of ingenue roles in Pittsburgh theater for 31-year-old actresses, either, I suppose."

Debby shrugged.

Beverly dropped back onto the loveseat. "So you got married and moved to Iowa."

"Something like that." Debby sipped her drink.

"Sounds good to me." Beverly lifted her glass toward Debby as if in salute, gulped half the contents. "The roast is almost done, by the way. Ten more minutes. Fifteen, tops."

Debby stared into her drink. "I could have gone back to doing the weather."

"But I needed her. I needed her to take care of me." Joe grinned.

Debby raised her lovely eyes to his pock-marked face. "You're my baby. You and Chekky."

"You should have real babies." Beverly's words emerged slurred by gin.

"Everybody should have babies. Kids make the world go round. Ha!"

"That's not an option," Debby murmured.

"Why not? Chicken?" Beverly barked a laugh.

"Female troubles. I had a hysterectomy, just before I met Joe. That's why I was so glum."

"I didn't care." Joe rested a big hand on his wife's knee. "You were the most beautiful woman I had ever met. Still are." Debby placed her small, soft hand over his.

Beverly shrugged. "Hell, you aren't missing anything. My kid's a little bitch, if you want to know the truth."

Head leaned back against the window, she stared at the ceiling.

"They all go through phases," offered Tess. "When Liza was four, I thought we were going to have to put her in an asylum. They get better. Erica will get better."

Beverly lifted her glass without tilting her head from the window. She maneuvered the drink to her lips and emptied it, eyes still on the ceiling.

"Nah. The kid takes after her old man."

She lowered the glass to the seat cushion. Her eyes slid shut and she toppled sideways, going down slowly, majestically, like an Oregon fir felled by a logger's saw. Her torso landed on the loveseat's cushion, her head on its arm. Her legs sprawled open and the crinoline-supported skirt flared, exposing pantyhose encasing dimpled white thighs and voluminous blue underpants.

"Is she all right?" Doug asked.

"She's asleep," said Debby.

Joe shook his head. "Passed out. She was bombed when we got here."

Tess gestured toward her hostess's slumped form. "Fix her skirt. It's embarrassing."

Doug frowned. "I'm not touching her. What if she woke up?"

Tess crossed the parlor, tugged at Beverly Nichols' dress. Her effort had little effect. Rearranging the skirt modestly would require rotating the woman's lower half and stretching her out, but the loveseat was short and Beverly's legs were long, so that didn't appear feasible. Tess planted her hands on her hips, pondered her hostess's condition.

"Hello, sweetie."

Debby spoke from behind Tess, who jumped, startled. She peered at Debby, followed her gaze to the hall doorway and discovered Erica.

Erica glared.

Tess looked at Debby. "Maybe we should take her to bed."

"Leave her alone," Erica snapped.

Liza stepped into the doorway, carrying a Barbie doll in a wedding gown. Her large brown eyes studied the scene.

Joe rose to his feet. "Your mother doesn't feel good, Erica."

"Don't touch her," the girl said. "She doesn't like it."

The couples exchanged looks.

"What should we do?" asked Doug.

"We haven't eaten," Debby said. "She invited us. The roast."

Joe hooked a thumb at Beverly's unconscious form. "She's in no shape to eat."

Tess sighed. "Maybe we should just leave."

"Yes," hissed Erica. "Go."

Doug and Debby rose. Uncertainly, the four adults edged toward the front door. Erica snatched the doll from Liza's fingers. Liza shot the other girl a frightened glance, scurried to her mother. Tess gripped her hand.

As they descended the walkway to their cars at the curb, Tess said: "Should we call somebody?"

Doug shook his head. "Who? Her ex-husband in Peoria? Derek Cahill? I don't see anybody who'd be much help."

"I think Erica has dealt with this sort of thing before," said Debby.

They all stopped, gazed back at the house. Then they turned away, climbed into their cars and drove off.

The Coopers traveled two blocks in silence before Liza asked from the back seat: "When are we going back to Oregon?"

A Gift Rejected
Michal Ann McArthur

"How come you're not fat anymore?" I asked Karen. When did that happen? Was she fat last week? I couldn't remember, but about half of her was missing.

Karen snorted and gave me one of her big-sisterly smiles. "You can't be fat and be a rock star. Obviously. Besides, Turk doesn't like fat girls."

Well, I figured he liked Karen plenty. He drapes himself all over her like a worm on a peach. She sings in his rock band on the weekends. She wants to be a professional singer, but Dad says she can't earn a decent living that way. I'm not so sure he's right. Karen brings home tons of cash from her gigs, even a one hundred dollar bill once. She let me touch it before she hid it in her suitcase under her bed. She says as soon as the weather warms up, she and Turk are hitting the road for New York City. Dad says she's unrealistic and childish. She says Dad doesn't know what he's talking about.

I was perched on the edge of the tub keeping her company while she got prettied up for her rehearsal. Not a gig, a school concert. She'd been chosen to sing a solo in "Silver Bells." I didn't even know she was in the choir until she told me about her solo. I can't imagine having the nerve to sing in front of hundreds of people. I'd probably pee my pants.

I watched her dot in her contact lenses like an expert. Her long black hair, straight and fine, fanned across her V-shaped back. Her clear face reflected back at me in the mirror, so smooth and white, she reminded me of Grandma's porcelain pitcher with its gold handle and hand-painted red roses. A family heirloom, Mom's pride and joy. I guess it was about the only nice thing our family ever owned.

Karen dabbed Shalimar on her graceful neck with the tip of her long white finger, and I gave my stubby fingers a dirty look. I'm dark, short, and sturdy like Mom. Once three or four years ago when I was still a little kid, Karen pointed out that I was built just like Laura Ingalls Wilder. That made me feel better.

I liked the way Karen's white floor-length robe rustled as she moved, the satin robe she'd bought on sale at an expensive department store downtown. Dad had given her money for school clothes and she'd come home instead with this robe and gold slippers. He was furious.

When Dad gets mad, it feels like the dictionary has exploded in your face: words, words, words, all carefully and precisely e-nun-ci-ated (one of his favorites). He used words on Karen like "impractical" and "wasteful," his face getting redder and redder. He pushed and pushed, trying to force her to admit she was wrong, but she refused. It's amazing how stubborn Karen can be when she's under attack from Dad's blast of words. She's the only one in the family who can stand up to him, including Mom.

"These are school clothes," Karen argued. "Having pretty things helps me feel confident in school." She sounded strong, but I could tell from her face she was about to cry.

Karen wouldn't take the robe back, and Dad said he wouldn't give her any more money. She said she didn't want any. I saw Mom try to slip her a twenty-dollar bill for shoes, but Karen pushed it away.

"Dad prowls through the house like a red-eyed grizzly in April," Karen complained to me. "He hates me. He and Mom have rejected me and criticized me all my life." Karen often said stuff like that to me. "Nothing I do is good enough for them. They're cold and angry and punitive." She had my sympathy, but I wondered what Mom and Dad would answer back in their defense. I think they'd deny it, especially Mom. Of course, I'll never know because they don't talk to me the way Karen does.

I puzzled over all these arguments and accusations as I watched Karen outline her lips in red. Mom hardly ever wears makeup and I don't know how Karen learned, but she's a pro. With her tiny brushes and pots of color she can turn herself into drop-dead gorgeous. "You coming to my concert?" she asked, blotting her lipstick on a square of toilet paper.

"Sure, if Mom or Dad'll take me. Aren't you nervous?"

"I'm scared to death."

I think Karen's the most honest person in our family, even more honest than Dad. I reached out and she took my hand. "I'm going to miss you when you go to New York City," I said, looking up at her.

"I'll miss you, too. But you can come visit. I'll take you to Coney Island and we'll have a blast."

I pinched off two shiny green needles and crushed them between my fingers. I love that sharp, strong scent. Our Christmas tree stood more than six feet high with thick branches all around—no gaps anywhere. What a prize! I helped Dad pick it out and get it all set up in its metal stand. My twin brothers, Dylan and Dallas, were supposed to help, but mostly they just got in the way. I stepped back to admire our work, bits of bark and sap sticky on my fingers. Mom talked about a family tree-decorating party, but Dad said, "Nope. I've done my duty. You kids decorate it. I'm taking your mother out for dinner and a movie."

When Mom hesitated, he said, "If you don't go with me, I'll find some gorgeous blonde who'd like my attention."

She said, "Oh. Well, in that case . . ." and got her coat. I figure it's only right that they should spend some time together, but it seems like we never do anything much as a family. It's either the kids and Mom, or Dad and Mom, but never all of us together. I guess that's because the only company Dad enjoys is Mom's. I don't understand why, and it hurts my feelings. He must think we're boring.

After Mom and Dad left, Karen and I got to work. First we untangled the strings of lights and wrapped them around the tree and then, when Karen was finally satisfied, the fun part—hanging the bulbs.

Peter lay on the couch, throwing tinsel at the tree.

"Come on, Peter," I begged, "won't you help?"

"I'm doing the tinsel," he said with a sly grin, glancing sideways at Karen.

I think he might have been trying to make her mad. Or maybe he was just having fun his own way. Dylan and Dallas copied Peter and started throwing tinsel, too. Karen frowned at all three of them but didn't say anything.

"Come on, guys, do it right," I pleaded. I wanted the tree to look nice, but mostly I didn't want Karen to get upset.

"Hey! This is the best tinsel job you'll see anywhere," Peter said, wadding up a glob and lobbing it into my hair. I pounced on him and gave his ear a fake tweak.

"Stop it! Stop it! You're hurting me," he howled.

I knew he was only kidding. "Say 'uncle,'" I demanded, twisting a little harder.

He grabbed my wrist and forced me to my knees. "Uncle," he groaned, stuffing tinsel into my mouth. I landed my elbow in his ribs and he let me scramble away. "You've killed me," he moaned as he clutched his ribs. "I'm telling Mom and Dad when they get home."

"You'd better not," I threatened, "or you'll find yourself with a fat lip."

"Oh no, please, not that," he said with a pretend whimper and fired another wad of tinsel at me.

I glanced over at Karen. Her eyes burned bitter, hollow and sad. She turned away and went back to hanging bulbs. She and Peter don't horse around much. When they fight, it's always for real. Karen has a small white scar above her eye where Peter hit her with a rock, and Peter has a dark spot between his shoulder blades where Karen stabbed him with a pencil. Dad has spanked them more than once for fighting, so they usually only fight when he isn't around. I don't understand why Peter "despises" Karen (her word for it) or why Karen drives him crazy with her constant criticizing.

When I saw that hollow look in Karen's eyes, I shivered. I didn't feel like decorating the tree anymore. But I kept at it. I didn't want to abandon Karen.

The twins got bored. Karen wouldn't let them hang any of the breakable bulbs, so they started begging for a snack. She told them to wait until we finished the tree. They wandered out to the kitchen and clattered around. I saw Dylan climbing up the cupboards.

"I'll be there in a minute," Karen called. "We just have to get the star on top."

The next thing we knew, we heard a terrible crash. We rushed into the kitchen, and there on the linoleum lay Grandma's white porcelain pitcher with the gold handle.

Shattered.

We were all stunned speechless.

"No, we can't glue it back together," said Dad when he and Mom got home and Karen showed them the fragments.

Mom's face went pale but she didn't say anything. Not a word.

"Can't we buy a new one?" said Karen.

"Don't be silly," Dad said. "We'd never find another one. And even if we did, we don't have money for things like that. I'm sorry, but those are the facts."

"We could check Replacements.com. Maybe it wouldn't be too expensive," Karen pressed.

"I have five children to feed and get through college. I said no and no is what I mean. I don't think you even know the price of a pork chop these days."

"But—"

"Throw it away and be sure the floor is swept up properly. Next time do a better job of watching the boys. This shouldn't have happened."

Karen cried herself to sleep. She tried to hide it, but I could tell.

The next few days around our house felt like somebody died. I dragged through the days with lead in my legs and arms. Even the twins didn't shout or get rowdy. They seemed to understand that their accident was a family catastrophe.

I buttered my second helping of roasted potatoes and heaped more baked apples and pork onto my plate. "When's your concert, Karen?"

"Next Wednesday night. It starts at seven. You're all invited to come if you want to. I don't want you to feel obligated. If you don't want to come, don't." She stared around the table at us all, her head erect.

"Well now, sweetheart, do you really mean that?" Dad reached for the plate of carrot sticks and picked off a handful. "Wouldn't you like us to come for your sake?"

"I don't want you to come just for me."

"Of course we will," said Mom.

"Only if you really want to," Karen insisted.

"If you want us to come for your sake, we'll come," Dad said. "But let's be honest, Ellen. A high school choir isn't what I'd choose to hear. We'd only go because Karen wanted us to go."

As Dad spoke, I cringed.

"Then stay home." Karen abruptly left the table with most of her dinner still on her plate.

The house shook as a winter storm struck with fury.

Dad and Karen were fighting in the kitchen. I huddled on the couch, trapped in the living room. I wished I could run away, but it was freezing outside and an icy wind rattled the windows. I couldn't escape without my coat, but it was hanging in the utility room, just beyond the kitchen. No way was I going to walk through the kitchen.

I didn't know how the fight started. Maybe Dad had been on the prowl and Karen had gotten in his way. The fight was a bad one, though, and I had this horrible feeling it would end in disaster for Karen. She was standing up to him, as usual. Too outspoken for her own good—that's what Mom said about Karen.

I heard Dad blast "infantile" and "foolish" at Karen. "Money" and "music" were mixed in there, too. He said, "You don't know how to wait for the right time for the right thing," something he'd already said a zillion times, but this time he sounded so ferocious that I felt mauled and I wasn't even in the same room.

Karen yelled between sobs and frantic catches of breath, "You're selfish and tyrannical. Why do you think you're always right? Why do things always have to be your way?"

I shriveled. I knew she'd gone too far. How did she dare face him, his thin lips pulled tightly together, his blazing eyes? He really did look like a red-eyed grizzly in April.

"I'm the boss in this house. I'll not have you talking like that to me. As long as you live in my house you'll do as I say."

"That's just it," Karen answered back, trembling, pacing around the kitchen, her face on fire. "We always have to do it your way or we're out. You think you're always right, like you're the only one in this family who counts. We have to agree or we're out. Well, I won't agree with you. You're the one who's wrong. You can't see things any other way because you don't want to."

Dad grabbed a kitchen chair and shoved it against the wall. "You've stepped over the line, young lady. I'm not going to have it." As he spoke, he unbuckled his belt.

I tried to shrink to nothing. I heard a hysterical sob catch in Karen's throat.

I stared at those long white fingers pulling the leather belt from its loops, and I shook all over, sick. I froze, the kitchen chair shoved against the wall in full view.

"Pull down your pants," Dad commanded.

Neither of them said another word. Dad arranged himself on the chair and pulled Karen across his lap. She was so big she didn't fit. He had to squirm and wrestle to get her positioned right. Then he struck her with his belt again and again.

The stinging cracks made me tremble. I squeezed my eyes shut and wanted to put my hands over my ears, but I couldn't move. I wasn't like Karen. I'd do anything to avoid being hit like that. Inside, I felt like a whimpering dog crawling on its belly. I thought I might throw up.

Karen broke the silence with an inhuman bellow. I shot up and bolted out the front door.

Two days later, I found Karen curled up on her bed, completely naked. Blue and purple bruises crisscrossed her bottom. "I'm fat," she moaned.

"You are not," I answered. Was she crazy? Her ribs were practically sticking out. "If you lose any more weight, you'll look weird."

"Turk doesn't like fat girls."

"Well, he should like you, then."

"I don't know. I don't know if anybody likes me."

I would have said, I like you, but I didn't think I'd count. At that moment, she looked thin and fragile and almost see-through, like a bone china plate. I thought of Grandma's pitcher. I didn't want Dad to shatter her accidentally. I worried that there was something already wrong with her, like she was already cracked.

I didn't say anything to anybody, though. I didn't know exactly what to say, and I didn't want to get her in trouble. But at odd moments that sad, hollow look in her eyes scared me. Sometimes, I was tempted to go right up to those eyes and say, "Who is that in there? Is that you, Karen?" I worried that the answer might be "No."

On Christmas Eve, we sang "Jingle Bells" and other songs with Dad at the piano, had cookies and hot chocolate, and went to bed. Finally, I thought as I shivered under my blankets, we actually managed to do something together as a family. We kids never believed in Santa Claus—Dad insisted on the truth right from the beginning—but I was still excited about what felt like the magic of Christmas.

In the middle of the night, an uneasy feeling woke me up. I rolled over to check the glowing dial on Karen's alarm clock: nearly three o'clock. My eyes searched for a lump in Karen's bed. No lump. I choked as though a claw grabbed my throat; my heart somersaulted in my chest. Where was she? She's probably just in the bathroom, I told myself, but I got out of bed cautiously. Maybe she's sleepwalking or filling the stockings. I felt my way down the dark hall to the bathroom. The door was cracked open, and I gave it a nudge. Yes, I could see Karen in the glow of the nightlight, on her knees in front of the toilet making a gagging noise. Then she threw up. I put my hand over my mouth at the sound. Poor Karen. Sick on Christmas Eve. How awful.

I stood without twitching. I didn't know whether to speak to her or not. I had the feeling that maybe she'd want to throw up in private. Finally, I decided to go back to bed. When Karen came in I'd sit up so she'd know I was awake. We could talk if she wanted to without her knowing that I'd seen her in the bathroom.

I tiptoed back to the bedroom. I waited for what seemed like a long time but by the clock was only about fifteen minutes, but she never came. I decided that maybe I should check on her. Maybe she was so sick she'd fainted or something. But no, when I peeked into the bathroom, no Karen. My scalp itched all prickly as I inched down the hall, heading to the kitchen and living room.

Halfway through the kitchen, something moved in the dark. Somebody was in the living room. My eyes strained to make out a shape, sweat trickling along my hairline.

Suddenly, the Christmas tree lights blinked on, and I could see Karen sitting on the floor in her nightgown, her back to me. With her legs curled under her, she looked small, like a little child. She began quietly opening gifts. As she worked, the tree lights reflected off the silver and red foil wrapping paper scattered on the floor, making the whole scene seem eerie and unreal. She was making a soft high-pitched sound, and I realized she was humming bits of her solo, the solo nobody in the family went to hear.

I didn't know whether to speak to her or not. I wasn't even sure she was actually awake. Why was she opening her presents? Was it because she couldn't wait till morning? Was Dad right that she was infantile and couldn't wait for the right time for the right thing? Or was there something crazy wrong with her?

Finally, I sneaked back to bed. I lay in the dark until Karen came. I sat up, but she didn't say anything. After awhile, I closed my eyes and went to sleep.

In the morning, I padded into the kitchen to find something to eat while I waited for everybody else to get up. When I threw away my orange peels, a bit of pink in the trash caught my eye. I shoved aside some garbage and uncovered a crushed pink bakery box, the kind cakes and donuts come in. The kind we never have at our house. Where had it come from? Why was it hidden in the trash?

"This year I get to play Santa Claus," Karen announced. She was dressed in her white robe and gold slippers, her hair brushed silky smooth, with just a touch of red lipstick on. Even though I'm her sister, I have to say, she looked beautiful.

"I think it's Peter's turn, though, isn't it?" said Mom gently. I could tell that she didn't want a fight to start. Peter shrugged. Apparently, he didn't care.

"I got to be Santa last year," I said, trying to support Karen's dibs. I studied the gifts under the tree, all wrapped exactly the way they'd been before Karen unwrapped them in the night. I searched Karen's face, but I couldn't find any clues in her eyes. She seemed normal, too, not at all sick.

"Well, does it make any difference as long as the job gets done?" said Dad. "Why don't I do it?"

I knew Karen felt stomped on by the way her face fell. I didn't want the Christmas spirit killed, so I said, "Can you say 'Ho, ho, ho,' Dad?"

"I'm the best ho, ho, ho-er you ever heard, my wild-haired piglet."

As soon as Dad finished passing out all the gifts, everybody dug in.

"Open your gift from me," Karen urged. "I can't wait for you to see it." She placed the package in my hands, her eyes sparkling.

I wanted to rip open the box as fast as I could, but I made myself ease the red bow off and tuck it into Mom's bow box and then remove and fold the wrapping paper neatly so we could use it again next year. When I finally lifted the lid, I found a snuggly lemon-yellow sweater, just like the kind the popular girls in my class wore, just like the kind I'd wished a million times I could have and never dreamed of asking for.

Karen looked hugely pleased with herself, and if I'd given a gift even half that great, I would've been crowing to the world.

For a moment I couldn't even speak. "Thank you," I finally managed to say. "I love it. It's perfect. How did you know?" I buried my face in the soft mohair.

Karen clapped her hands and laughed like a little child. "So, you like it?"

"I love it."

"Is the color all right? I think it shows off your dark complexion."

"It's perfect."

"You never even suspected, did you?"

"No. Never." How I wished I'd bought her more than a box of stationery and a pair of gloves.

Mom and Dad unwrapped a large heavy box, their gift from Karen. Karen cuddled up in her satin robe and watched them. All the gifts to her lay beside her, still wrapped. I suppose she wasn't in any hurry to open them because she already knew what was inside.

"Can you guess what it is?" Karen's purr was so loud I could almost hear it.

Mom shook her head. "No, I can't imagine."

Dad cut the heavy strapping tape and pried off the lid. He dug through the shredded packing paper.

"Careful," Karen said, "they're breakable."

He held up a delicate white dinner plate edged in gold. Mom gasped.

"It's a complete set," Karen said. "There's even a meat platter and a soup tureen."

"But Karen," Mom protested, "this is fine bone china. You can't afford to give us a gift like this."

"I don't want you to save it for special occasions. I want you to use it every day and feel special. It's a setting for ten so you can have company, too. That band's real gold."

"But," Mom said, "bone china's fragile and expensive. It's not for every day."

Karen brushed away Mom's protests with a happy wave of her hand. "Dad, this gift's for both of you, not just Mom. I tried to pick a pattern that could be masculine or feminine. Unwrap some more. I want you to see the cups. The handles are gold."

By this time, Peter and even the twins had stopped opening their gifts and sat perfectly still, watching. Everybody was quiet.

"I think we'd best not," said Dad, his lips thin and tight, his face stern. "These dishes must have cost several hundred dollars. You can't give a gift like this, sweetie. You mustn't."

"Our old dishes are good enough," Mom said. "I appreciate what you've done, though. Maybe we could each keep a cup and saucer or something."

"Nope. Send these back," said Dad. His hands shook as he wrapped the plate in its heavy gray cardboard and placed it back into the box.

He was really mad, but I couldn't understand why.

Roughin' it in Style

Astroturf is Forever
Matt Young

Dust sticks in my eyes as I drive the unimproved county road through Zionsville, Indiana to the Zionsville Lutheran Church where Julie Olson's funeral has already started.

A foggy myopic lens shrouds the windshield and filth splays from the vent system, filling the cab of my stepfather's truck with haze. I can taste it on my tongue and feel the grit between my molars. I breathe in the staleness. The Indiana dust coats my lungs, along with dust from the hills of California, from airport tarmacs, and foreign deserts.

The grime cakes to my dry lips and I remember what it's like to live in that earth. How we got to know it so well all some guys did was take pictures of the sand, family photos in the endless Syrian Desert. We relied on it for shelter against incoming mortars, or firefights, but there was no escaping the heat. I could never get deep enough. We were always digging, with shovels, and boots, and hands, searching for some kind of relief, trying to find the end, like we were digging our own graves.

Three days ago, I was in California, sleeping off a hangover, when my phone rang. It was my mother. Early calls remind me that she doesn't think much of a job that doesn't require me up before noon. Her ulterior motive is that I'll be too hung-over, or too drunk to realize that I've agreed to come home.

I held the phone to my ear as her disembodied voice berated her co-workers, the Indiana weather, and distant family members. I walked to the bathroom to empty my bladder, leaving the phone on the comforter.

It's been years since I've come home. So long I can't call it that anymore. Indiana is just a place I lived once. I make excuses at holidays that I don't have enough money, that I can't find a dog sitter, that I'm working on a story and can't make the time to leave.

When I left, it was like I pressed pause in my hometown while my life kept going on elsewhere. No one knows me anymore, so it's still a decade ago and I'm eighteen to them. They see the kid that got caught smoking outside the mall when he was sixteen, or that crashed his car into a fire hydrant, or that cried if he got tackled too hard playing football. I've stopped trying to change their minds. If they think you're the same old screw-up, then they don't feel bad about never having gotten out of town themselves. Inevitably ninety percent of conversations with old acquaintances go like this:

So, did you kill anyone over there? Are you alright? (Concern, or sympathy). Jesus, I, uh— What're you going to do with a degree in English anyway? (Sad, disbelieving headshake). Hey there's lots of— I guess you could always be a teacher, that's pretty much it, right? (Crossed arms, look of smug satisfaction). Well actually I'm a writer. Writer, huh? What do you write about? (Incredulity, inability to be impressed). I chronicle the lives of people who can only have orgasms while dressed in mascot costumes. (End conversation)

In truth, I write slam pieces about local celebrities for a magazine in Dana Point, California, aptly named The Dana Point Dish. I write stories with headlines like, "So-and-so's Daughter Seen Exiting Planned Parenthood" or "Local Weatherman Caught Cheating: Forecast Calls for Divorce." Trash writing for a trash magazine. Come to think of it, telling people the truth of what I do for a living would be enough. Thinking about my job makes my own stomach turn.

As I returned from the toilet, I prepared myself for the onslaught of guilt about never visiting. I put the receiver back to my ear to the sound of my mother's disappointment in the rapid decay of her own body.

"...and my knees are so bad, I can hardly walk the dog anymore. Just the other day your father was telling me—"

"You mean Kevin?"

"Yes, Kevin. Anyway he was telling me that I should maybe try and get the congregation to pray on it. He thinks maybe it will help."

My stepfather is a local televangelist on late night public access. After my parents divorced, my mother became an insomniac. Said even though she couldn't stand my father's drinking and gambling, she couldn't sleep without him next to her. She made a lot of late night calls to Kevin Allstott's Faith Revival, to talk and pray about her situation. Mainly, she told me later in confidence, to speak to the handsome man on the television. I don't know if my mother is a believer, but the one thing she doesn't complain about is how she sleeps these days.

I didn't give an opinion on the matter of divine intervention for the sake of her cartilage, but instead offered a thoughtful, "Huh."

"Well that's not the only reason I called." Her voice sounded tentative and I braced for the waves of shame I would feel after her multiple uses of the word "abandonment."

"Mom, it's five in the morning. Five-fifteen now."

"You remember Julie Olson? You two dated. I liked her, you know. She was very nice."

"Yeah, Jesus, I haven't thought of her in years. How's she doing? If she's single I'm not interested. You realize I don't live there anymore right?"

"Jimmy—Jimmy, she died yesterday. It was a car crash in Bloomington."

"She teaches art down there the last I heard," I said. There was silence on the other end of the line.

"Well—I thought you should know, the funeral is in three days—I wanted to tell you that I love you."

"Love you too, Mom." I tried to go back to sleep, failed, and packed a suitcase.

***

Julie and I had gone together during the last year of high school and the summer before college. I went to her house almost every night after work, driving down the highway at youthful speed, trying to reach the exit for Zionsville before I had to pull out the headlight knob. Julie and I swam in the pond behind her house or sometimes I would go fishing with her father, Jack. When it got dark, her parents and the two of us would play cards late into the night. Later, I would drive home smelling of catfish, burnt skin, and pond water.

I remember her wearing a white bikini with cherries pasted all over it, standing on a bright green pontoon in the middle of the water, waving to me and smiling, dark hair wet and plastered around her tanned face. Sometimes, I wouldn't bother taking off my clothes, but would run, crashing into the pre-dusk calmness. I could hear her laugh just before I hit the water and then my clothes would vacuum against my skin as I glided beneath the surface. We would sit with our legs dangling in the water, catfish nibbling our toes, watching the sun fall in the sky.

I lost my virginity on that pontoon, after the sun went down one night.

Her skin, still warm from the day, felt smooth and firm under my newly formed calluses. I wanted to press into it, to live there and never be cold again. The Astroturf her father had carpeted over the wood rubbed the skin raw on both my knees. It was fast, and I was clumsily reluctant to take my mouth from hers. The mosquitoes were heavy over the lake and the breaching catfish sounded like golf balls falling around us. At the end of it all, I noticed my swim trunks had stayed around my thighs the entire time.

Mosquito bites covered my back the next day, and my knees cracked and bled whenever I bent them. I reveled in every drop of blood and every itch. They meant that I could never go back.

She went to Indiana University to study art at the end of that summer. It was a two-hour drive and we broke up. I saw her once after that, before I joined the Marines. She was home for fall break and had called, wanting to see me. It was the first time I'd heard from her since she'd left. I said I would meet her at the pond around dusk, but instead waited until after dark to show up. She said hello and I responded with my plan to join up. I remember that she cried, telling me I was a fool to go and fight that war. I said she was pathetic, that at least I was going to do something with my life. I told her that I was happy to go. That I would stay in for twenty years and kill Iraqis the entire time and be goddamn happy. And that's how I left it. I walked away from her, her family, the pond, Indiana.

Ten years later here I am. The gravel road ends in a rocky parking lot full of American-made cars. A simple white church looms against an azure Midwestern summer sky. I pull into an open spot and shut off the ignition. The temperature rises and blood pounds in my ears, but I stay where I am. The white doors open and people in dark suits file out. I can see sweat glistening on the foreheads of the pallbearers as they step into the heat. The casket is as white as the church, so white it blurs my vision and I can't stand to watch it any longer.

The parking lot is siphoning out in trace of the hearse. A man and his family in the car to my left motion for me to go ahead and pull out, but I wave them on instead. He looks annoyed and backs out with purpose, flinging rocks in my direction. I don't go to the burial.

Instead, I drive into the Zionsville countryside, through fields of corn and soybeans, along more unimproved county roads, hunched over the wheel, straining to see what's in front of me.

I drive past the rock quarry where I used to smoke dope with my friends in high school. We jumped from cliffs into the dark depthless water during the height of the summer heat to the cadence of cicadas in the treetops. My old middle school is there, long darkened and condemned, merged with another township. The playground where Kenny Farcas knocked my front tooth out and Donald Frye stood up for me, blackening Kenny's eye, looks rundown. On the long stretch of road between the old school and the highway exit is Julie's house. I pull into the horseshoe driveway and park by her father's tool shed.

I walk to the pond, past the small ranch-style house where I spent the evenings playing cards and making out with Julie on the couch in the living room after her parents went to bed. The soundless glow of the television set, turned down for fear a parent would wake and come to the adjacent kitchen for a glass of water, cast elongated shadows throughout the room. We kissed with the kind of urgency only teenagers seem capable of mustering; hands forever searching for a firm hold, mouths form-fitting to one another, heads angled, eyes closed. I peaked sometimes, when I kissed her neck. She looked caught in a kind of heaven and I would think that it was because of me.

The grass has been freshly mown and cuttings stick to the cuffs of my jeans. The small rowboat Jack and I fished from is still anchored by the pea-gravel beach. I helped Jack shovel that gravel from his truck one day, and afterwards we sat on a handmade bench by the shore and he gave me a beer. Jack had an easy manner, a farm boy to the roots. We talked about fishing and what I was going to do when the summer ended. He talked about scholarships, but I closed him out.

"I've already got a job," I said. I worked at a shipping company then and I thought that it wouldn't be so bad to stay there. I was earning ten dollars an hour, more than any other kid I went to school with.

"It's an honest job," he said, staring over the pond. "That's important, you know? Having something honest that you can be proud of."

I nodded, happy that I pleased him. I waited for him to say more, but he didn't. He smiled at me, a little sad smile, as I got up and walked to the house for the nightly card game.

I think now that maybe Jack saw the next ten years unfolding before him when he looked at me. Saw Julie go to school, saw me get fired for drinking in the parking lot during break, saw Julie argue with her mother and him about going to school for art, saw me turn to the military and all the rest.

I sit on that same bench now, sweat pooling into the neck of my tee shirt, the sun heating my face as it makes its descent. I want to dig, find a cool spot, save myself, and I scoop a handful of pea gravel into my palms, letting it sizzle. More of the small stones move back in its place. I'm on my hands and knees now, the hot gravel burning my palms, trying to move enough of them to make a hole to squeeze myself into. A slurry of gravel dust and sweat covers my neck and arms and I try scraping it off with my fingernails, but it won't come.

I tear at my clothes until they're piled around me. Sweat streaks my burning skin. I look up and there's the pontoon. Still there. I blink, trying to focus, my lids scraping the lenses of my eyes. The sweat on my exposed skin dries in the swelter of the remaining day and tightens my body. Naked, I walk into the pond. The surface is lazy and still. It's too hot to bring the big fish to the surface. Reaching waist deep I go under. I dive down, skimming the bottom. My ears pop. The water is cold here, and dark. You don't have to dig in the water, you can just disappear. I can feel the filth slough from my skin. I open my eyes, irrigating the haze.

My lungs strain and I break the surface three quarters of the way to the pontoon. Ripples go out across the water, causing the platform to bob and rotate gently. The green of the Astroturf is untainted. It glows brilliant in the shimmering heat, and I wonder if Jack replaced it. Or maybe Astroturf is forever. I freestyle the remaining length to the silver four-rung ladder hanging from the raft, and pull my dripping body onto its surface. Chest heaving, I splay to the four corners. The plastic is fiercely hot, but I force myself to lie still. Water trickles off my face and into my ears, dulling languid birdcalls and the steady slap of water against the barrels keeping the raft afloat. I close my eyes, and wish for the mosquitoes to come out.

Transmogrify
Nyla Alisia

A utilitarian glass bubble, misshapen, stress-cracked, impact-chipped, broken loose from the fisherman's net, singly, becomes something altogether different, when floating alone, reflecting that twilight-universe between water and sky, lost in a swirling nest of mystery and sea-foam.

A Well Matched Man
Chelsea Bieker

His timing was cruel. Ephram decided he would leave Bee within twenty-four hours of her mother's death on a black ice warning day in December. They had been together nearly a year, but he had contemplated ending it for a while. There were lists—pros and cons, short-term and long-term. He held their photos up next to each other and noted that her weak chin and downturned eyes would mar his dominant bone structure and perfect brow line. Their children could potentially be unattractive. He had been tentatively planning a spring break-up, in time for the eager rush of skin to peek out from strange women's warm-weather halter-tops and above-the-knee skirts. He had plans to meet someone quieter with larger breasts preferably at a sidewalk café. Together they would drink carafes of sangria and consume dainty plates of un-fried appetizers, maybe a nice ceviche in a cocktail glass, and he would bask in the warm and wonderful buzz of relief at having gotten rid of Bee, his hanger-on.

This didn't fall in line with his plan, but it was perhaps more efficient, he thought. She would be too distraught over her mother—who had been run over by a semi-truck on a wild and horribly-timed sprint across the road to the Steinmart—to feel the full effect of his absence. He didn't want to be around for her nose blowing, return to drinking Charles Shaw with Sprite (why did she always insist on cheap wine?) and inevitable weight gain. Bee was an emotional eater. The more comfortable she got in their relationship the more she ate, and pre-mother's death, she was already coating perfectly healthy snacks—apples, celery, sprouted grain crackers—in nut butters. What would happen with the onslaught of a new and unknown type of depression? He simply did not want to know.

To Ephram, the idea of guilt was a vast inconvenience, and it was what had kept him from ending things sooner. Guilt frightened him, and made him feel unsure of himself, something he didn't have time for. He had always been an out of sight out of mind kind of person—the opposite of Bee perhaps, who was romantic, and spoke like they were acting out scenes from quirky love story movies at all times. He knew that she would be the sort to throw things, beg, scream, and sob. He knew she would inundate his phone with take-me-back-texts and they would probably engage in post break up sex. But when she had called Ephram with her terrible news—the solution became clear. He was on his way to her apartment to make a clean break.

Ephram entered Bee's collaged, cluttered space and found her sitting on her hideous vintage couch, her un-lipsticked mouth slurping liquid from a plastic cup. He knew it. A bottle of two-buck Chuck sat half-empty on the coffee table. She didn't hold up well. After a big cry (which happened at least monthly) Bee always resembled someone fresh from a heroin detox, the tore-up-from-the-floor-up kind of thrashed that was puffy and smelled like sour milk. He checked his reflection in her entryway mirror. Even-toned complexion, dark lashes guarding his two surprisingly aqua eyes. He smiled for a moment to reveal a straight row of squared white teeth. Later, he hoped, when Bee accessed how things ended, she would remember how polished he looked in the midst of chaos.

"What took you so long?" Bee said. "I need you right now. This is the shit I'm talking about."

"Babe, I'm really sorry about this," he said. "How did she not see the truck?"

"How many times do I have to tell you her depth perception is off," Bee said. "She was going there to get me a shower curtain."

"Why can't you get your own shower curtain?" Ephram was often confused by Bee's family unit who seemed interested in doing mundane tasks for each other.

"How could you say that?"

"Have you called Ellen?" Ephram wanted to make sure Bee had an arsenal of support for when he made his escape. Ellen was her best friend who wore a horribly severe pageboy bob.

"Yes, she's on her way."

"I know this isn't the best time, but I think we should talk," Ephram said.

"Actually I have to tell you something. I'm just going to do it and get it over with. It's terrible. Are you ready?" Bee stood up.

"No, are you ready? I have the terrible news."

"I'm in love with someone else." Bee put her hands on her hips.

"I really think I should be with someone more on my level," Ephram said over her.

Bee threw a plump velvet pillow at him. "This is my moment. I am breaking up with you. I've been having an affair with Fionne."

"This is not your moment." Ephram stood up and stepped closer to her, pointing in her face. "Fionne is a bull dyke."

"You're not even hearing this," Bee said. "I want you out of here."

"I came over to tell you we're finished," Ephram raised his voice. "You're eyelids are far too droopy for someone your age."

"I really loved you," Bee said. "I don't know why. My family hated you. My mother, God, she really hated you."

"That's not true," Ephram said. "Grandmother Peach said I was beautiful like a woman."

"That doesn't mean she liked you," Bee said. She slumped back into the couch. "My eyelids are droopy?"

"They can probably be fixed," Ephram offered. "I should go."

"For the record, I initiated this break up, not you."

"Fionne. How long?" Ephram asked.

"Just a few weeks," Bee said. "I thought we might get married so I wanted to try to be with a girl. But then I realized you're a shit."

"I can't picture it," Ephram said. "She's not suitable for you. Why not Ellen? Ellen has a nice shape."

"You are so fucked up," Bee said. She poured another spritzer. "Get out so I can mourn my mother."

"I really think it was me who broke up with you, though," Ephram said. "I can show you the lists I've been making for proof."

"Get out."

Because Ephram had been banking on a spring break-up, he hadn't properly prepared to meet the future mother of his children (he was thirty four, it was time) in the dead of winter when rain fell in sheets of ice and it was impossible to properly take stock of a woman's body because of thick, fluffy down waterproof coats and hideous puffer vests in colors like minted sage and bold burgundy. Goddamn REI. He paced the aisles of the grocery store steering an empty cart. He wore a sleek all-weather Burberry trench, belted at the waist so not to mistake his svelte form. But what about you, hot blonde reading a magazine in aisle twelve? I can't see your tits under that godforsaken North Face rain jacket two sizes too big. Or you, nicely scented Julia Roberts look-a-like in bakery line. You could be a size two, but I can't see your ass when what looks to be a shoddily knitted sweater belonging to your grandfather is tenting it. Fuck's sake. And then, there was Fionne at the meat counter buying slabs of beef back. Her curly dark hair had grey streaks and he wondered if any part of her was contagious. He had slept with Bee only last week. He cringed.

"Fionne." Ephram tapped her shoulder. "I'd like a word."

"I don't have a lot of time," Fionne looked straight ahead at the butcher packing her dead animal.

"I just want you to know that you didn't break me and Bee up. I broke up with her."

"When Bee described you, I told her there was no way someone was that terrible, but already I can tell she wasn't exaggerating."

"How is she anyway?" Ephram eyed the translucent chicken breasts lying in slabs atop one another.

"Her mother just died, so she's not good. I'm making her dinner tonight."

"That's a lot of meat."

"I freeze it. It's on sale."

"Tell Bee not to contact me," Ephram said. "Tell her I'm moving to Los Angeles."

"Good riddance."

He walked away from Fionne and her broad shoulders, abandoned his cart and got in his car. Los Angeles. As soon as he had said it, he realized it was the only thing to do. He had had it with this place. He would move and put these past three years of purgatory behind him. He recalled living in sunny Las Vegas before Oregon, and how things were easier there. In Oregon it seemed people walked around in a haze of organic farming and community bike shelters. Coffee emanating from their breaths, huddling outside of art galleries engaging in slam poetry. It had been a rough three years for him, and if someone suggested a hike to Mt. Hood one more time, he would be the one to run out into the road in front of a truck.

The handsome allowance he received from his father and his well-paying job offered the whimsy of moments-notice freedom. To Los Angeles! Where the sun shone on the regular, and Santa Monica was swarming with hot girls on rollerblades on their way from their hair appointments to the beach. And Bee hated Southern California.

With the help of his father's endorsing phone calls, Ephram easily lined up a job as a financial planner at a prominent firm and flew out the following week, leaving most of his belongings on the street for the homeless, or more likely, starved hipster free pile Craigslist scavengers. On the plane he practiced flirting with the woman across the aisle, and she blushed furiously. When she smiled he noticed her teeth were crooked, but if she kept her mouth closed she was all right. He enjoyed the game of watching women melt under his attention.

It should be noted here that Ephram was every bit as smart as he was good looking, his brains a back up ticket for when women of ranks six or seven became shy around him at bars. He would play it saccharine suave, add in a bit of clumsy quirk, and be in their panties by the end of the night. His normal strategies hadn't worked with Bee, though. In fact he hadn't done any of his normal moves on her. They had met toward the end of Ephram's off year when he had worn braces. He had been depressed, hadn't made many friends and worked too much. They were hired around the same time at the same company and were both new to Oregon, and could commiserate over the weather and the strange people. Of course, in no time Bee became one of them, getting a job at a co-op and taking up pottery. In retrospect, Ephram blamed his weakened self-esteem for why he opened up to Bee and let her know him in a way he had never let anyone before. They would stay late filing slips of paper, and he would tell her about his mother who had killed herself when he was twelve, and the subsequent parade of nineteen-year-old sluts his father ushered in after her death. He told her about lying awake in fear that he would wet himself, because the one time he had, his mother called him retarded and forced him to sleep in his own dampness. Through these confessions, Ephram began to rely on Bee in a peculiar way. He began to find her frizzy brown hair inviting, like cotton he wanted to put in his mouth. Watching her reach up to the highest file drawer, the way her little flat shoes would slip off the back of her round pink heels—it gave him a rush. In some Oedipal miscalculation, he had asked her to dinner. The plane landed, and Ephram collected the phone number of Emily. Under her name, he penciled in, "crooked teeth" to remember her. He knew he would never call.

Ephram spent the weekend getting settled in and on Monday night, he parked his new Jag into a spot outside of The It on Sunset to meet his new boss, Slade, for cocktails and handshakes. The bar restaurant club was a swanky place, a place Bee would have never been let in the door. As a woman, to be admitted into The It there was a base requirement of hotness, something he appreciated for its downright convenience. Not a one of them was wearing a single piece of unsightly outdoor gear. Hips and tits and cellulite-free thighs swarmed around on expensive high heels specifically manufactured for sex. Bee had one pair of high-ish heels, which she ruined for him every time she told a complimentary stranger they were "organic comfort cork, my Grandma shoes!" Those, and the hideous mustard corduroy pants she would cuff around the ankles were enough to induce vomit. Thank God for real women, those with enough sense to forego boner-reducing casual wear. Yes, thank Christ for the women of L.A.

Slade was situated in a corner booth being helped to bottle service by a voluptuous Latina hybrid type with possibly the finest waist-to-tit ratio he had ever seen. Slade was a handsomely aged Ken doll, with salt and pepper hair gelled into place. Slacks crisp and tie loosened, he invoked an effortless sophistication. His nose was waxy as if it had been freshly sculpted from blemish-less clay and attached just hours before. He smelled rich like fine leather and Yves Saint Laurent cologne. Ephram wanted what this man had. Upon contact, his palms felt expensively exfoliated. Ephram thought of the photo of him and Bee he had found that morning unexpectedly in an old filing folder, and knew he would be mortified if Slade ever saw it.

"Ephram, so good to finally meet you, my man." Slade sat back down in the booth and ran his wedding-ringed hand over the helmet of perfect hair. "Your father has told me a lot about you—he's pretty excited you've decided to come out here—get out of that rain hole, eh?"

"It was time, it was time." Ephram wondered exactly what his father had said. It was surprising that he might have conveyed an "excited" tone, as he was possibly the most stoic man Ephram had ever known. "How long have you known my dad?"

"We worked together in San Fran, Jesus, I guess twenty years ago. It's been a while. He's a good man—a helluva business man, that's for sure. It'll be good to have you around, hopefully you're half as good."

"I'll do my best, sir," Ephram said, just as Latina Love Bomb came back with a plate of crisped asparagus and some kind of dip and told the men to enjoy.

"I'd like to get in on some of that," Slade said as he reached for an asparagus. "Maybe I will." He started laughing, and Ephram knew that was his cue to laugh as well, although he wasn't sure what was funny. Was Slade referring to the waitress or the food? For some reason he thought of his mother sitting in front of the television alone night after night with the same lavender crocheted blanket on her lap watching re-runs of Rosanne. He thought of Bee and her love of mismatched tableware from the Goodwill as he plucked a spear from the cobalt platter.

"Why not New York to work for pops?" Slade asked. "Just curious."

Ephram couldn't tell Slade that his father wouldn't hire him, not now, not ever. That his father had made it clear when Ephram had graduated college that it was best he keep his distance. His father did have a new family—had remarried and essentially started over, impregnating Gretchen, a woman Ephram's age, with twins. Certainly his father had helped him make connections, but he had no interest in partnering with Ephram or having him nearby.

"I'm more of a California man," Ephram said. "My father knows that."

"Of course, of course, well let's talk some business, then."

The first time Ephram and Bee had sex, he was fascinated by the way she squirmed under him making animal sounds he had never heard before. It was as if her entire body had relinquished control and she had entered into some other mode, one that was so surprisingly erotic and sexually inspiring that he literally had to think of baseball (that old cliché) in order not to come. As she was about to orgasm, her eyes shot open and looked into his and in that moment as he came too, he understood briefly what it might mean to be one with someone, to share something fully. The women he had been with before put on elaborate shows, rubbing their breasts and chanting dirty phrases, opening their legs and licking their fingers. Bee had her own routine, and while it may not have been flattering, he knew she was experiencing real pleasure. Occasionally she would do something weird, like lick his armpit, or make non-sensical noises in his ear, her own language. He supposed now that perhaps their sex life wasn't altogether bad. Bee had cute nipples, after all.

There were women everywhere. And not just any women—actresses, wannabee pop stars, aspiring trophy wives—there was something in their eyes that just screamed "put a ring on my finger!" Bee never talked much about wanting to get married. Instead she wanted to move in together, mostly because it was cost effective and they would be able to afford a place where she could plant a garden. Marriage was secondary. Bee was always trying to make peoples' jobs obsolete. Why garden when there is a natural foods store on every other block? Why knit your own ugly wool headwear and scarves when there were boutiques and shops that conveniently had them for sale? Ephram never told Bee how rich his family was, and the more time that passed, he could see it was as if she did not care, or factor his net worth into her love equation at all. Another reason she would make a terrible wife. Financially irresponsible.

So when he met Elle at a company party after only a month in L.A., and she held her lips slightly parted open at all times resembling someone in a constant state of awe, or a blow up doll, depending on your disposition, he knew he would ask her out, and possibly marry her. She was tall but not too tall, and her skin had this oiled-down tautness to it. She was tan and her black dress was sexy but not slutty and its open back revealed tattoo-free skin. He accessed that her tits were either real or incredible replicas, and her long sandy hair was lighter at the tips like she spent days on the sand under the sun. She was also mildly interesting, and he didn't find himself zoning out as she explained why she loved So-Cal and how excited she was to have gotten an internship at such a prestigious company. "Did you say you were twenty-two, Elle?"

"Yes."

"Oh, perfect."

A week after the party, Ephram sat across from Elle at her favorite restaurant ever, and tried to imagine her as his wife. She would eventually fall in love with him if she hadn't already, and he envisioned their engagement photos (on the beach at sunset, a few of those sillouetty type shots) and he felt elated at the thought of his father asking Cynda, their maid, to put one on the fridge. My son, and his beautiful wife, he would say to his guests. Gretchen would be jealous because Elle was a smidge more attractive than her.

"Elle, do you like vacations?"

She smiled to reveal her dedication to professional teeth bleaching. "Of course I do. Who doesn't? I want to go to Catalina Island for a few days, I've heard it's fabulous. Or I'd want to go on, like, a cruise to Cancun or something."

"All of that sounds lovely. I just have one question." She leaned forward in her seat a little. Ephram reached across the table for her hand. "Would you like to go to those places with me?"

"I would love that," she said. And as she turned her face to the side to greet the waiter setting their food on the table, he noted her absolutely angelic nose and complete lack of double chin. She took a small bite of her grilled chicken—can you make that butter free?—and he was, pretty certainly, in love and over Bee entirely.

But like a child who no longer feels excitement over a once epic trampoline, or a couple who eventually finds their ocean side cottage to be a normal un-breathtaking fixture of everyday life, after nine months, Ephram no longer saw Elle as a picture of perfection. For one thing, she wore quite a bit of makeup, and now that she was comfortable (why must they all get comfortable?), she would remove it before bed, and sometimes go whole days at a time without it. It might not be a problem if she remained well-complected, but she didn't, and she had an annoying amount of freckles and moderate patches of acne. He was also horrified to discover that her natural hair color was more red than beachy blonde and kinked around her forehead in these odd little tufts of spongy wires when she didn't flat iron it.

He lay in bed staring at her sleeping form contemplating her shortcomings. She had been living with him for the last three months and it was in this time he was truly able to see her for what she was, and it pained him to admit it—cleaned up white trash. He should have known that her celebriphilia (obsession with movie stars, a real disorder he had pored over on Google)—researching them, meeting them, taking iPhotos of them, sleeping with them—gave her away as someone from a weaker pedigree. The truly wealthy understand that one does not make a fuss if one sees a star. Most stars are new money varieties, and while they are accepted into the social graces of the old monies, there is still a protocol. When Elle explained to Ephram her fantasy of "running into" and seducing Channing Tatum— "I just know he would want me, like seriously, I know it. I mean, E, you understand, he is like my number one boink fantasy. Everyone gets one free pass"—Ephram nearly lost it. He restricted her from visiting the Channing Tatum fan site (on which she was a preferred user) and he made her burn her Tatum love journal, pages and pages of entries where she had logged his birthplace: Cullman, Alabama, his birth year: 1980, star sign: Taurus. Not to mention the page she had devoted to red-sharpie-demonizing his "disgusting pig-faced-bitch-wife Jenna" on which she had drawn X's over her eyes, and scribbled DIE across her chest. It seemed Elle had been keeping this journal for years. There was a list of "Channing Planning" techniques—places she would sit in hopes of running into him, cafes, clubs and bars. My God, Ephram thought, My God. She wept as she tore each page and set it upon the backyard bonfire. Ephram maintained a stone face glare as she begged his forgiveness. She had been very bad, and the next offence would have her out on her ass.

Elle breathed deeply in her sleep, but thank God she didn't snore like Bee. He reached over and brushed a finger over her long eyelashes. Well, no one is perfect, he thought.

"Elly, Elle, wake up."

"What?"

"Elle, have you ever worn anything from Patagonia?"

"What's that?"

"Never mind, come on, get up, lets go for a jog, you could use it, you know."

"I shouldn't have eaten those almonds last night."

"Sweetie, they were covered in chocolate. I mean, you just need to know you limits is all."

She rolled out of bed and reached her arms up in a stretch. He loved her back, so smooth and tan. He liked seeing her ribs when she strained.

"Elly, when will I meet your mother?"

"Why would you want to meet her, she's horrible."

"I feel like it will help me know you better, meeting your family."

"She's a hoarder in Booneville, Missouri and she's a miserable cow."

"Hoarder? What do you mean cow?"

"She collects thing, her house looks like the stockroom of a fucking Walgreens," Elle said. "And she's fat."

"You never said your mother was fat. Is she your biological mother?"

"She eats fried stuff and doesn't understand what a trans fat is."

Ephram felt his head might explode. Elle had mentioned her mother in passing. He knew she lived in Missouri, sure, but he had formed his understanding of her to be a charming rendition of Martha Stewart with an affinity to plaid aprons and front porch iced tea drinking. But fat and hoarder? This information really threw a wrench in the system. Bee's mother wasn't the brightest tool in the shed, she had been killed running across the street after all, but she had been running at least. She was fit, she went to yoga classes. Her hands were dry from gardening, but she counted calories. He started to shake. He looked up at Elle who was trying on various neon sports bras and he wasn't sure how he felt anymore. Genealogy was a strong current, one that you couldn't deny or change. Elle had sweated and smiled and saloned her way to L.A., but what about longevity? What about lineage?

"What's your dad like?"

"He's a cop, I told you that."

"Yes, but, what does he look like?"

Elle walked over to Ephram sitting on the bed and straddled him wearing the neon green bra and matching neon booty shorts.

"Well, baby," she said with an exaggerated southern twain, "He's a well-fed Missoura man." She started laughing and licking his ear. Ephram grabbed her waist, taut as it was, and threw her off him as if by reflex. Elle landed on the ground.

"What the fuck?" She asked.

"I'm sorry, I need to go."

"What is wrong with you?"

"Now, I'm going now. I need to be alone."

Sometimes, when Ephram was upset, he would call Slade. Slade had good advice, and always seemed to quote something his father had once told him. Ephram liked that, as he couldn't admit weakness to his own father. Slade's wife, Heather was beautiful in her late forties, and though Ephram knew that Slade found it difficult to remain faithful, he didn't think much of it after Heather had reached between his legs and felt him at a dinner party a few weeks ago. Maybe that's just how their relationship worked. Either way, Slade was a good man, and he knew how to live.

"Ephram! My main man. How's it going?"

"It's Elle. I have a big problem."

"Elle is a real looker, buddy, nice little body, that one."

Ephram paced away from the house. "That's the thing. This morning she told me her mother is fat hoarder and her dad is a well-fed cop."

"Oh, Jesus. How fat?"

"I don't know, she said her mom is a miserable pig. She lives in Missouri and doesn't know what a trans fat is. She sounds really, really fat."

"Listen, I understand man. Heather's mom is a total dog. I freaked when I first met her, but I think you can navigate this."

"How can my future kids have a cow grandmother?"

"Ask to see some pictures."

"I went crazy on her, I threw her on the ground."

"Ask for some younger pictures, if they look alike, you can bet Elle will follow
suit."

"Bee's mother was a runner. Before she died she ran a half marathon. Thirteen
miles!"

"If she doesn't look like the mom, you're in the clear, she will evolve in her own
way."

"Bee's whole family was emaciated, sure she ate when she was sad, but she
starved most other times!"

"Who is Bee, man? Who are we talking about here?"

Ephram would pour over his mother's journals after she died, reading line after line into her morbid reflection—his father ceased to find her sexually desirable after year three of marriage, her life was a series of disappointments, her own father had favored her younger sister, the world was terminally unfair, she had misgivings about being a mother, and so on. The most disturbing of the entries detailed the year of utter disdain she felt toward the infant Ephram. He specifically remembered the sentence, I can barely walk past his crib without feeling an overwhelming urge to lift him above my head and drop him on the floor. Ephram wished later in life he had never read the journals. Had he not, he might still be able to possess a comforting heartbeat of denial.

So Ephram knew it was a bad idea to rifle through the shoeboxes Elle kept in the back of the closet. He had a few hours until she would be home, and he needed to find photographic evidence that she was not a physical replica of her mother. Elle kept little things. Ticket stubs, notes from friends, coupons, cheap jewelry, broken pencils, awards, certificates—but photos were scarce. She had held on to a few small square images of awkward teenagers from her high school group of friends, the backs reading, "have a great summer," and, "C U next year!" He just needed an old family photo, that was all. But when he came across an envelope from West Hollywood Clinic of Plastic Surgery his heart raced. Elle was too good to be true, and the bills and paperwork documenting her nose and chin job practically wrote the conclusion to their brief affair themselves. He methodically packed her things into boxes and trash bags, there wasn't much, and set them in the driveway.

He called Bee.

"What?" she said.

"I need to see you," Ephram said. "I think we made a mistake."

Bee was silent for a moment. "A mistake is forgetting to pick up the dry cleaning, or using salt instead of sugar."

"Remember when we went to couples counseling?"

"How's Los Angeles? I hear you're engaged."

"I'm far from engaged, Bee. The therapist said I didn't honor you. I finally get what he meant."

"Enlighten me."

"I don't know. I've never been appreciative enough."

"What's happening? Why is your voice so high pitched?"

"I just need to see you," Ephram said.

"I never want to see you again."

"I'm going to call you back tomorrow and the next day and the next day—I'm ready to work through my past like you said."

"I don't believe this."

"Your eyelids are fine, I don't know why I said that."

But Bee had hung up on him.

Ephram walked to a nearby Coffee Bean (yes, technically a sidewalk café) and indulged in a mocha blast vanilla frappe with whip as he browsed his smart phone's photo library. He had never deleted the old images of Bee, and now reviewing them, her chin didn't look so weak, and her eyes were only slightly down-turned when she smiled. He recognized that her long limbs would probably be hard pressed to gain weight even if she tried, and her hair was more naturally wavy than frizzy after all. But what surprised Ephram the most, as he flicked through the frozen images of the only woman who had ever known him, really known him and loved him anyway, was that he deeply missed her. He missed her in a way he had never felt, not even when he discovered his mother dead in the bathtub, and the years he spent mourning her late at night, crying softly into his pillow. He missed Bee because though she accused him of being superficial, and their fights usually orbited around the fact that she would not throw away her foul smelling pairs of burlap Tom's shoes, she was willing to stick around for the best of him, the side that wanted to be a better man, the Ephram who gave her a rose for every month they were together. The one who actually felt horribly sad when her mother was run over, but couldn't figure out how to properly deal. He decided he would call her again tomorrow, and every day there after if he had to. The sun blazed down on him and his eyes ached. How he missed the overcast skies, driving to the rocky coast, eating deep fried funnel cakes at the state fair. He felt pain that Bee had cheated on him with Fionne, but he couldn't blame her. While he had been making lists and staying up late into the night on photo composite websites predicting the bone structure of their future children, of course she had sought affection elsewhere. And now they were the same, their mothers decomposing in the ground of the earth. They were alone, each of them. He scrolled to his favorite photo of her, walking down the street in a halter-top through a weekend farmer's market. He had been trailing behind her, snapping artistic pictures. She turned around and he caught her most genuine smile. Her tattoo was showing, it's branches reaching up over the line of the sheer blouse. He had never told her, but in that moment, as she examined eggplants and conversed with the vendor, he had found Bee's tree to be very interesting, and once he had gotten used to it, quite beautiful.

Criticism
Rick Stoddart

Words pursed in -
four-walled rooms
long
and
high-ceiling-ed,
pigeon feathers
in the corners,
a chair made of broken bones
upholstered in
ruby red fabric
sits center,
very center -
centered… here.
This place
a jaunty silence
dancing and covering
impropriety with chalking plaster
creativity becomes secret
individualized in tiny boxes
deep inside each nerve ending.
Criticism, then
always dragging
furniture into every building
rearranging – redirecting
oxygen and airflow
until breathing is
no longer your own
process.

A Permanent Marker

Rick Stoddart

Cite the item.
Score the rock.
Graffiti is a breadcrumb
from life to landscape.
I know you.
I know this…
Touch a hand to the "this".
A lingering fingernail
Passing over — against.
The grime caught
underneath, is its own citation
for detailing day to day
a meaning of your very own,
built by calculated concrete
and a most beatific paint.
This is yours.
This you know…
"this-ness."
A new wrinkle in the brain
lost among hair and context
only seen in the last autopsy of your life.
This, you'll never see
but only envelope
like a piece of art
or a reminder
left by a forgotten culture
spoken in the same shocked whispers
encountered in a darken cinema.
You are the artifact,
the pocket knife,
the spray can of paint.
The instrument — self-referring.

If I Wore Sensible Shoes

Ginger Dehlinger

If I wore sensible shoes
would I choose the road most traveled,
wait on the curb for the walking green
and shun the slippery slope?
Would I walk past the rogues and scoundrels
to stand by the man with intelligent eyes,
or conquer the corporate ladder,
rung by treacherous rung?
If I wore red, peep-toe stilettos
would I learn to tango and dance all night with a gigolo,
or walk along the Seine with a stranger
who fed me snails and sweetbreads?
Would I flash my toes at the Met
and in the shops along Fifth Avenue,
feigning surprise when I saw myself in Vogue
or on page 6 of the New York Post ?
If I wore lunar-tech, racer's edge athletic shoes
I would dare to rush the net on a clay court,
hike the west rim of Zion,
and leap across the Seine with Michael Jordan.
I would blaze my own trails,
outrun the rogues and scoundrels,
and at the end of a Wonder Woman day,
cool my burning feet in an icy mountain stream.

Egret on the Willamette

John Byrne

White
No compromise
Stark
White
Against the winter dun
Of bankside bark and leaf-fall brown
Still
White
Above the mud-brown swollen stream
Sheer
White
Slash
Sudden
Down
And from the ripples raised
A grey-brown squirming fingerling
Up-ended
Shook
And swallowed down
The pure
White
No compromise.

Turn That Pioneer's Eye

No Curtain. No Scenery.
Sarah Angleton

We had a sold-out crowd that night. That meant one hundred and fifty people all crammed into skinny metal bleachers, legs pressing against the person next to them, each spilling slightly over the space allotted by two thin lines of worn green paint and a stenciled number.

I picked him out of the crowd right away. My husband Craig sat, just as an avid theater enthusiast might, right in the front row, smiling his charming smile and speaking with a young pregnant woman next to him. I knew why he was there, of course. In the three years I had been involved in community theater, he had never once shown up, and, in fact, I hadn't seen him at all in that time. But over the past few months he had begun to call. Just the occasional quick, casual message at first, saying that he had some news and needed to talk to me. Then more frequently, his voice taking on a frantic edge. "I really need to talk to you, Jenna. Please give me a call," He would beg. I never picked up the phone. And then he showed up at the theater.

I've always been curious why people come. Why, for instance, would a wealthy looking man in a full suit and too much cologne, choose to spend his valuable Saturday night in the front row of the latest disgrace of an otherwise beautiful play?

I mean, there was Nick who occasionally announced that he had single-handedly filled a third of the seats. "I offered extra credit to my history students," he would say, proudly, as though we should all be grateful that our audience had been coerced into suffering through our pathetic attempt at art. But as for the rest of the crowd, I wondered why they bothered

Occasionally I would discover the answer, maybe in the cast meeting after the performance. Andrea would say something like, "Did anyone notice that my father came and sat in the front row? In a suit no less! Bastard!" I'd always nod sympathetically with the others and wonder if they knew why this seemingly supportive, if a tad bit overdressed, father was such a bastard. No one ever asks. We all know what it's like to face a demon in the front row.

Or at least now I understand.

Sometimes I think I am the only one who gets that at the end of the show when we take our bows, people applaud because the agony is finally over. If they stand it is less for our acting brilliance than it is for the head start they hope to get to the parking lot in order to avoid the need to greet the cast members with some congratulatory comment or hilarious witticism.

Maybe I'm being too harsh. We aren't all terrible. Hailey is a theater major at the university and works with us on occasion. She has some genuine talent. Her boyfriend Scott helps out sometimes, too, and has a pretty decent voice so we try to cast him in the lead for all the musicals.

The rest of us, I suppose, have our moments. I did have one particularly stunning performance as Mary Magdalene in Jesus Christ Superstar last spring. In my more optimistic moments, I imagine I sang like a wistful songbird and gazed longingly into the eyes of my Savior, played by a guy named Ed who works as a high school janitor and has long blond hair so he kind of looks like Jesus, although he can't sing to save his soul.

So that's what I hope for. A few glimmering spots in a sea of graceless theatrical blunders. Like that night. We performed Our Town. It was the last of five weekend performances. We always do five: two Saturday nights, two Sunday matinees, and one Sunday night. Sunday performances bring in the biggest crowds because church groups are generally good for community support and, frankly, pity.

I played the lead. We have a kind of rotation. Andrea, Jules, Kari, and I are the four main female players. Then there's Hailey who fits in whenever she is available, which isn't often because she's usually busy with a better a show. We like to say she is our official understudy because if she can be there, then it is our duty, we feel, to be too sick to perform.

There was one time when Sally Thompson, the local news anchor, decided to try her hand at community theater so we let her be Eliza Doolittle in a low-budget, scantily cast production of My Fair Lady hoping that the combination of her semi-celebrity and the musical's popularity would draw in a bigger crowd. It didn't. Sally never wanted to do another show with us after that.

So it was my turn to play the female lead (Emily). And my demon was in the front row, with his very pregnant girlfriend.

Emily Webb, who later becomes Emily Gibbs, is a fresh-faced sixteen year-old innocent with a robin's egg blue dress that matches both the color of her eyes and the ribbons at the end of her long chestnut braids. Or so that's the way I imagine her. I, on the other hand, am a sad forty-year-old with gray streaks in my hair and permanent bags under my eyes. I do this because without it I have nothing more than a dead-end receptionist job and a lonely apartment. Even with a lot of makeup, I am a depressing Emily.

Our Town has just the right balance of theatrical merit and gushing sentimentality to appeal to our church-going, community oriented demographic. But primarily we chose it because the first stage directions are "No curtain. No scenery," which is perfect for our small warehouse theater since we don't have a curtain, or even a real stage, and have next to no budget for scenery.

Most importantly, Our Town is a tear-jerker, even poorly performed making it easy for us to feel a sense of accomplishment watching a crowd filter out of the auditorium, sniffling and wiping moist cheeks. Even though I don't look much like a convincing Emily, I was more or less pleased with my performance through the first four shows. And that night, as Craig sat there watching our last show, I thought that if I could maintain my focus on the play itself, the energy of it would be enough to see me through whatever he had in store for me.

As the lights dimmed, I peaked around the black plywood partition that forms our backstage area, and I could see Craig's silhouette just beyond the spotlight shining down on Harold walking slowly onto the stage. Harold, an insurance salesman in real life and the "stage manager" in the play, cleared his throat and delivered his opening line: "This play is called Our Town and it is written by Thornton Wilder."

I got through my first scene just fine. Jules and Kari squawked their way through their morning breakfast routines as overbearing mothers and everyone followed their leads pretty much on cue, which was something of a miracle since there are two separate conversations going on at once on different areas of the stage and for nearly a month of rehearsals Todd (George Gibbs) had consistently participated in both.

But it was when stage manager Harold called to the front Professor Willard to give the history of Grover's Corners, that I let myself get distracted. I glanced into the audience and once again I could see Craig's outline, sitting straight (a career military man, he prided himself on his perfect posture), and holding the hand of the woman next to him.

She looked pretty, this woman, who once had been me. Her shadowy silhouette was slender, except for the bulging belly, and she was neat and proper with her ankles crossed and tucked in front of her. I knew he had been seeing someone; rumors had told me that much, but it was still a shock to see them together, and I hadn't known about the baby. Obviously this was the reason he had been so desperate to talk to me. He wanted to move on— had moved on it seemed.

We'd been married eighteen years: thirteen mostly good, two sad, three separate. It started as a classic story really. We got married right after I graduated college. I was twenty-two, he was twenty-one. Some would say we had been high school sweethearts, but I've never been a big fan of that phrase. It makes sensible people with genuine attachment to one another sound like foolish children. Yes, he was hard to live with, impossible to talk to at times. He wasn't a bad guy or anything, just never one to express very much.

About six months after we got married, his older sister Rhonda came to live with us for a while, pounding on our apartment door in the middle of the night, her stuff piled up in her Chrysler. Her husband had gotten drunk and beaten her, so as soon as he'd passed out she'd left with everything she could carry. I suppose most brothers would have been out of control with rage, probably gotten in their cars themselves and rushed to their sister's defense, and maybe part of him wanted to, but instead, Craig just quietly helped her unload her car, put some sheets and blankets on the couch and went back to bed.

He tossed and turned the rest of the night and for several after, looked terrible in the mornings, but never said a word. I don't think he knew how to talk about anything, not with his sister, and not with his wife.

"Psst." A frantic whisper ripped me from my memories. Kari, a stay-at-home mother of three who confessed to doing community theater in order to escape her kids for a while, glared at me. "Jenna, time to go!"

"What?" I said, startled into the present. She pointed to the stage.

Harold was beginning to panic, talking loudly and slowly, as if he were speaking to a confused old man who didn't hear very well. "It's later than I thought. There are the children coming home from school already."

I pulled myself away from my memories and with all the dramatic power I could muster, tripped onto the stage. I delivered no line. Instead, I looked right at Craig, and not with the sixteen-year-old innocence of Emily Gibbs, but with the hurt and sorrow of a grown woman whose innocence was long gone.

What followed was the first of two big scenes with Todd when Emily helps George with his algebra as a pretense for romance. I think I must have mumbled most of my lines. Truthfully it wouldn't have much mattered if I didn't. Todd would have gladly performed the entire scene as a monologue. Besides Hailey, who might actually have a shot, Todd was the only one of us who ever considered himself a real actor. He claimed he'd even auditioned for a few Broadway productions in New York, though without success. Now he owns a deli downtown and lives out his dream in the largely ignored Glendale Community Theater where he consistently steals lines, convinced he never has as many as his talent warrants.

I responded appropriately when Todd said, "Hello, Emily."

Then it starts to get a little fuzzy. Todd continued, "You made a fine speech in class."

I looked at him, blinking in the lights, and said, "Thanks." But that was not my line.

Todd glared at me and then, smiling, made an awkward attempt to cover. "I know you had prepared to make a different speech and the teacher changed at the last minute. You must have worked really hard." Here he paused, signaling, I guess, that he had finished my line and was about to launch into his, which, I assume, he delivered flawlessly. I don't know because all I could think of was the last time I had seen Craig.

It was the day he moved out of our little house on Oak Street. We had been fighting about the money in Jared's college fund, what to do with it. All we did in those last two years together was fight. Jared's death could have taught us to talk to one another, but instead, all that emotion that should have been shared grief, came out as anger. That was the day we finally broke.

Looking back, I'm not sure why we stayed together so long after it happened. I guess we felt like we owed it to Jared somehow, like even a dead child would be better off if his parents were married. Three years later, the money in the college fund still hadn't been touched. Like our marriage, it stood as a permanent memorial to our son.

I moved out of the Oak Street house two months after Craig left, as soon as I could convince myself he wasn't coming back. When the movers came to pack up the boxes, I told them to put everything from Jared's room into a rented storage unit I've not visited since, hired a cleaning service, put the house on the market, and moved into the apartment building next to the theater. Truly alone for the first time in my life, I needed something outside of work to pull me back into the world and around people. I started performing later that year.

Craig and I communicate through lawyers if at all. He never gave me any grief about the house. He never filed for divorce, and neither did I. The last thing he said to me was, "Don't forget to feed Ernie." Ernie was Jared's goldfish. I actually don't know what happened to him. Maybe he's floating, dead in the storage unit.

I don't know how many of my lines I managed to choke out during that scene with Todd. I had been running those lines for so many weeks that I should have been able to do it on autopilot, but when Harold announced intermission and we all filed back behind the partition, the look on Kevin's face told me I hadn't done remarkably well.

Kevin, a middle school English teacher with a flare for the dramatic, directs most of our plays. "What are you doing out there, Jenna?" He asked, in a harsh whisper.

"I'm sorry, Kev," and I really was. I was sorry to be ruining the show for the others. I was sorry that our audience had paid to see me screw it up. I was sorry that I was so affected by the sight of Craig in the audience.

I sighed, "My ex-husband," then I corrected myself, "sort-of my ex-husband is in the audience tonight with his pregnant girlfriend."

Everyone had been looking at me accusingly when Kevin first addressed me, but now there was a fresh energy to their concern, like a fierce alarm was sounding in their heads. No one spoke for several seconds and all that remained audible was the low mumble of the crowd on the other side of the partition.

Andrea was the first to speak. "Bastard!" she said, and the others nodded in agreement even though none of them knew anything about my life and had no idea what it meant for me to see Craig there that night.

"Sit down, honey," Jules spoke in a reassuring motherly voice and put her hand gently on my shoulder. I could only assume she still drew this from her character because ordinarily no one would accuse Jules of behaving motherly. She works in a state welfare office where she spends her days breaking the hearts of desperate people and her crusty edge follows her into her personal life.

I sat down on one of the folding chairs that would be carried out in a few minutes to set the stage for George and Emily's wedding. Kevin brought me a Styrofoam cup of water, staring at me while I drank it.

"Will you be able to go back on?" he asked, probably more concerned for the performance than for my emotional state.

I reassured him. "Kevin, I'm fine." That wasn't true, but I was determined that it should be because, after all, I had spent the last three years of my life consciously ignoring that fact that Craig was ever important to me so I thought I could certainly do that for at least one more night.

"Just give me a couple minutes. I'll go out there and make you proud." Kevin nodded, cautiously satisfied, then made a broad sweeping gesture with his arms, encouraging everyone to back away, as much as our cramped quarters would allow.

Fifteen minutes later, Harold began, "Three years have gone by. Yes the sun's come up over a thousand times..." and the second act began.

I didn't look at the others during the wedding scene because I kept trying to see Craig and the woman. This close to the spotlight, it was difficult, but there were times when the focus left Emily and went to other characters and at those times I could catch a glimpse.

I admit I should have been concentrating on the play. I had promised Kevin and the others I would, but my thoughts drifted instead to the two of them sitting together in the darkened front row. She was the reason he needed to talk to me. Finally, it was going to really end. It was just like Craig to get his girlfriend pregnant, but remain married to his estranged wife. That way he could hold everyone at a safe distance and his life wouldn't have to be so wrapped up in emotion all the time.

I supposed she must have forced the issue. She probably told him that he needed to make a meaningful change in his situation. Maybe this woman had finally gotten to him in a way I never could. In a way no one ever had.

I remember thinking, while pretending to sip ice cream sodas with Todd, I didn't look that good when I was carrying Jared, not even half hidden in the shadows. When George asked Emily to be his girl and she (I) said "Yes," I was looking at the woman now holding my husband's hand

and wondering if she would make him happy. I realized I wasn't jealous of the affection Craig felt for her as much as I was jealous of the love she seemed to feel for him.

Moments later when the play cut back to the wedding scene, my gaze again fell on Craig as I spoke my first line to Kevin who was playing double duty as both director and Mr. Webb because we never had enough men.

I said, with heart-felt sincerity, "I never felt so alone in my whole life. And George over there, looking so…! I hate him. I wish he were dead."

Maybe I really did hate Craig as I spoke. I hated him because even though we had gotten married too young and never managed to figure out the secret that every other married couple seems to know, I didn't quite know how to live without him either. And I hated him because not knowing the secret to marital bliss meant that when Jared was thrown off his mountain bike into a tree, dead on impact, Craig couldn't help me figure out how to live without our son.

I kept my word to Kevin, though, and somehow transcended these thoughts, plowing almost gracefully through the act. When Harold, with a bow, said, "Curtain," the audience clapped politely, Kevin flashed me a grateful smile, and George and Emily Gibbs walked hand-in-hand off the stage.

We only had about a ten-minute intermission after the second act. It was just long enough for the stagehands (any of the actors who didn't have a quick costume change) to rearrange the wedding folding chairs to be the gravestones for the third act. We didn't want to make the break too long because, by this point, we feared the audience would be growing tired of our performance and, given the opportunity, might choose to leave.

I put on my third-act dress quickly so that I could return to the stage and help with the chairs. My help wasn't really needed, but I wanted to see if I could catch Craig's eye, to see the kind of read I could get from him. He must have been anxious to get my attention, too because as soon as I stepped out from behind the partition I heard my name.

"Jenna!" A little stunned at hearing him address me after three long years, I acted as though I hadn't heard him at all, but he was persistent. Louder, he shouted, "Jenna!"

I turned to look in his direction, careful not to pinpoint him too accurately. "Craig?" I asked, squinting into the semi-darkness. "Is that you?" I walked slowly toward the front row of seats.

"Hi, Jenna." The woman next to him politely turned away, suddenly fascinated by the paper maché comedy and tragedy masks hanging on the wall to the left of the stage. "The show is going great. You look good up there."

Craig was never a good liar, but I thanked him anyway. "What are you doing here?" I asked him.

"I wanted to talk to you, Jenna. I thought maybe in person would be best. You know, after the show. Maybe we can go for coffee or something."

"Jenna, we're going to get started!" Harold's voice called behind me.

I looked back at him and nodded, then once more, just a glance really, at Craig before turning to go. He looked so nervous, like a little boy about to confess to breaking his mother's favorite lamp. It occurred to me, looking at him in that moment, how lonely he must have been all those years, just like me. The lights dimmed and his face became little more than shadow. I hurried to the folding chair awaiting me on stage.

The third act was my least favorite. It was the sappy, sentimental kind of mush I hated, but no matter how awful the performance, it was the act that made the audience cry, and so we ended on an emotionally draining high note.

So it's strange to admit to myself that on that night, as I acted my way through Emily's emotional epiphany, through her grief at realizing that life slipped away much too quickly without a single person taking notice, it got to me a little. I couldn't quite place what it was at first, but by the end of the final act, when Todd fell prostrate at the foot of my gravestone folding chair, I found that I was crying right along with the audience. And when Harold wound his watch, saying, "Eleven o'clock in Grover's Corners. You get a good rest, too. Good night," I was, maybe for the first time, proud of our little amateur troupe.

Hidden behind the partition, as the crowd filed out, I paused for a moment, trying to imagine how I was going to face what Craig had to say. After Jared died I'd tried to start over with someone else's life, the life of a person who had never lost a child. Somehow, I'd needed to be Emily Gibbs, the woman whose baby lived while she died and I could see how Craig needed to be someone else's husband, someone else's father.

And as I thought about leaving soon to meet the other actors at the bar, I found that whatever Craig had to say, it no longer mattered.

Mary Lou's Make-Over
Mike Ritchey

Mary Lou stood at the kitchen sink, looking out the dirty window at a blank and endless landscape. In the far distance, a row of long-empty grain silos formed a hazy skyline against threatening clouds.

Used to be something, this place, she thought, wiping her wet hand over her head, adding a shine to her black hair. "People? Water?" she said. "My God, Chub, this time of year? There was a time spring would come and the land turned green, as far as past forever, a smooth carpet of green."

Mary Lou dropped a dishtowel on the counter, rolled the sleeves of her khaki shirt down and buttoned them at her wrist.

"Ruined now though," she said. "Dry as a bone. West Texas. Gone plumb to hell."

She looked a moment longer out the window then stepped past her husband, Chub, slouched in a ladder back kitchen chair. He wasn't talking. She opened the screen door, leading onto the rickety back porch.

"I'll be back when I get damned good and ready," Mary Lou said and laughed. "And when I do, you better be right here, waiting."

Outside, she tapped her boot against a loose board on the step and called back into the house, "You've just about finished it off, Chub," she said. "About all we got left is what you're sitting in." Mary Lou shook her head. Here I've put up with it all this time, she thought. As much my fault as his.

She looked away from Chub's dog, Buck, as though she would walk past him, then kicked him with her booted foot, catching him full in the side. Buck, a big, gray mongrel Chub found at a farm equipment auction several years earlier, yelped and scrambled backwards off the porch and along the side of the house.

Mary Lou bent to pick up a small rock. Buck turned and ran around the corner of the house and sat there, out of sight, whining. Mary Lou threw the rock against the house near the spot she knew the dog was hiding. It bounced off the wall, taking a part of the dull green asbestos siding. Mary

Lou, a former center for the Wayland Baptist Flying Queens, stood six-feet-three inches tall and easily carried one hundred and ninety pounds. She had played softball and basketball in high school and college and though more than two decades had passed since those glory days, her throwing arm had not lost its zing. She reached down to pick up a larger rock, and fired another high hard one. It banged off the house, dislodging a full panel of asbestos, which shattered when it hit the rock-hard ground.

Mary Lou stepped away from the house toward the barn. She walked with a limp, the result of Chub's failure some years earlier to brake the old John Deere as he pulled a dead cow from a borrow ditch and—with her straddling the ditch and yelling at him to stop—backed one of the tractor's huge rear tires over her leg, breaking it at the knee.

"Too bad about the knee," Chub had told her. "But you're old enough to know how to behave around machinery."

It was an early chapter in a sad story. She wished she could have read the whole book right then.

Limp or no, Mary Lou walked fast, her long arms stiff and swinging at her sides. She heard a faint and familiar "pop" in the knee and winced from the slight pain, as she kicked the rotted tire of a motorcycle, half buried in sand. Chub bought the motorcycle with money she'd saved from the sale of an armoire that had belonged to her grandmother. She planned to spend the six hundred dollars to overhaul the motor on the well. At the time, traces of water remained—water enough, she thought, to inspire another crop or two to rise from the ground.

But Chub had taken the money from her secret hiding place beneath the feed trough in the corral. Her father built the trough when she was a girl, raising calves to show at the county fair—her project in 4H Club.

A blue ribbon every year, by God, Mary Lou remembered, her hands on her hips, looking at the vacant corral. "Let's see," she said, speaking to herself, "there was Prim, Dimples, the steer I had, Big Boy ..." She paused, pursed her lips. Some more, too, she thought. All of them had done real well.

But one afternoon while she was in the shower, Chub had left in the pickup truck and had come back with the motorcycle late the following day. When she confronted him, he laughed and said he'd known about the hiding place all along, but waited 'til she'd saved what he needed. Chub rode the bike all the way to the first flat tire. The machine, blown over by the wind, would be covered completely in sand in another year. The yard had been lost for years.

Inside the barn, Mary Lou grasped the handles of a rusted wheelbarrow loaded with partially disintegrated twenty-five-pound blocks of salt. Like the motorcycle, the wheelbarrow had not moved in years. Its tire, too, was without air, but Mary Lou, straining, slowly pushed it out of the barn and a hundred feet or more away from the house. She walked back into the barn and found a short length of rope. Back at the wheelbarrow, she called to the dog. All she could see was his head, poking reluctantly from behind the house.

"Come here, sweet boy," Mary Lou said, cooing. "Come on, puppy." She squatted and held her hand open, softly snapping her long fingers.

Buck, his head drooping, his tail between his hind legs, walked slowly, carefully, toward her. She clucked at him, as though he was a horse. When he got close enough to touch his nose to her hand, Mary Lou grabbed him by the collar, stood, and kicked him again, harder this time, then tied him to the wheelbarrow with the rope.

"Can't have you running off now," Mary Lou said, picking up a handful of dirt and throwing it on the dog. "You lie down with Chub, boy, you're gonna get up with more than fleas." She reached down to rub the big dog's ears. "Hang in there, Buck," she said. "We're almost to the anchor leg."

Back inside the barn, Mary Lou folded her arms across her chest and looked up. She could see the sky through the holes in the roof. Over the years, rain and wind and, more to the point, a lack of timely attention had resulted in the loss of as many as a fourth of the roof's wood shingles.

She hadn't known. Her head back, she raised her arms, clenched her fists, and, looking through the roof at the cloudless sky, she yelled, "Goddamn it. I just didn't know." She dropped her arms and closed her eyes. "How could I know?" she whispered. She held her face in her hands. Just big and ugly, she thought. Never even had a boyfriend.

She wiped her eyes on the sleeve of her shirt. She took a deep breath, unfastened the barrette holding her long black hair in place, and shook it loose, until it fell over her shoulders. She put the barrette in the pocket of her jeans. With her eyes locked on the stall in front of her, she set her mind free.

***

She thought of Whirlwind, the big roan gelding her mother and father had given her one Christmas morning. Mary Lou recalled that first time she saw him, his breath bursting from his nostrils, making that cold morning so different from all the mornings that had come before and would follow. Whirlwind. She had turned thirteen the end of November, just less than a month before her parents awakened her, blindfolded her, then led her, still in her pajamas, wrapped in her mother's blanket coat, out to the barn. Whirlwind.

"One hell of a Christmas," Mary Lou said, still looking at the stall. She'd cared for, ridden, talked to, and cried with the horse through high school and college. She spent even more time with him as he aged, after she came home from Dallas, leaving a job she had not been interested in. She'd come back to help her mother after her father died. By that time, she had abandoned any thought of marriage, not entirely with sadness or a sense of regret, to spend her life alone, on the farm, keeping it in the family.

"Oh, Mary Lou, Honey, you need a man around," former classmates would tell her, on those rare occasions when she saw them—reunions or homecomings, maybe the Fourth of July.

"If that's not the truth, I don't know what is," she answered. "You see one big and strong and dumb enough to have me, send him around."

"Well, Honey," her friends might say, "you've had your trials by fire, God knows. This is hard country."

Trial by fire? Hard country? Tell me something else I don't already know, Mary Lou thought.

Mary Lou imagined the conversations about her, and, really, she appreciated them. She knew that her friends loved her. She knew, too, they had what they felt to be her best interests in their hearts. Early marriages, children and church—theirs were the lives lived by their parents before them, and those before them, going back to their ancestors new to a difficult land.

If she hit rough spots, if she had concerns, worries, about being the last of her family, the end of the line, she kept them close, learning to absorb disappointments. It was just a life, she thought. She could manage. She could keep up the farm. And she came to understand—even to believe— that it was simply left to her to draw the last straw.

"And I sure enough drew it," Mary Lou said again. "The short straw. The runt of the litter is what I pulled out of that jar."

Mary Lou put both hands on the top rail of the stall and shook it. Be awful hard to prove she'd known much of anything. She kicked the back wall of the barn. Be awful damn hard to prove.

***

Three years after she settled back on the farm, her mother died. Sitting for hours and days at her mother's bedside, Mary Lou lost track of time. They reminisced and, when her mother's brain was not fogged, they laughed, too. Chores were put off, deadlines delayed. Her mother's death caused Mary Lou to slump into a sluggish mourning. A year, maybe fourteen months later, Chub showed up at her door.

"Passing by on my way to somewhere don't want me," he said with a laugh that mid-morning. He then nodded toward the corral where a rail or two had come loose, one end resting on the ground. "My time's my own, and I don't like to see chores go unattended. Might be you could use a little help for a while."

Chub was a small man with dark red hair and beard. Standing on the back porch, she towered above him. Mary Lou could remember how she had physically struggled to drag herself out of what seemed to have been a dream.

She had looked down at Chub. "I guess," she said. And without contract or further discussion, Chub stayed.

A sitting duck, Mary Lou thought, walking around and around in Whirlwind's stall, kicking every step or two at the dirt, the rotted old straw. Never had a date in her life. Didn't mean she needed just any little pissant man between her legs. She stopped circling. "Didn't need it," she said. "But that's what I wound up with."

Chub set up house in the barn, coming inside only once or maybe twice each day for the bathroom, an occasional shower. His work was not expert but sufficient. He seemed to be interested in maintaining the place. Now and then—a Sunday noon, then a Saturday, say—Mary Lou let him in for lunch or dinner.

"Don't know as I deserve it," Chub had said, turning his hat round and round in his hands. "Doubt any man would. I never expected a fellow could have it this good."

That was such a sweet thing to say, Mary Lou thought. No man had been so close to her before. And it seemed fair. After all, she was lonely.

She was prepared for her role—born and raised in the tiny house, miles and miles outside the nearest town, a half-hour's drive from even a distant view of anyone resembling a neighbor. Mary Lou was comfortable there.

***

The consummation of the marriage resembled the culmination of a siege. Mary Lou was six inches taller than Chub, and she thought his sounds and movements must be like those made by rutting trolls—weird, unknowable creatures, grunting and clambering through pages in the children's books her mother taught her to read.

She'd been thirty years old and a virgin—nothing to be proud of, she thought, but it might have been nice to have turned loose of it in some other way than she finally had.

It was not long before Chub's ardor waned from too often to more often than enough—the lack of energy, of interest, was also evident everywhere on the farm. When the well motor began dragging, Chub said it would be too costly to replace. No water meant no ground to plow, no seeds to plant, no cotton to raise. No more cows meant no need of pasture and a mile of ruined fence. The roof on the barn, even the house—and the house badly needed a new coat of paint—well, Chub said, "I'll get to it." And he added words she came to know by heart: "In my own good time."

***

When Whirlwind died, Buck was the last animal left on the farm.

"Whirlwind," Mary Lou said, scuffing the dirt floor of his stall with her boot, speaking aloud to hear the sound of his name. "You were one hell of a good friend to this girl."

But he'd died, just laid over, spent. The horse's death left Mary Lou alone. Pretty much over, she remembered thinking. It had all been pretty much said and done.

The night the horse died, she sat with a cooler of beer, alone in the barn, talking to him as he lay on his side in the stall. She sat all that one night then with the dawn she cranked up the backhoe.

With the front-end bucket, she rolled Whirlwind's body onto a heavy canvas tarp, wrapped and tied it around him, then dragged the body out past the little family cemetery. She dug a hole five feet deep and buried him there. With a hard chisel and four-pound hammer, she took two days to carve out "Whirlwind" in an odd-shaped, three-hundred-pound boulder she'd hauled from the dry creek bed that bordered the south side of her land.

Whirlwind.

***

"West Texas can kiss my ass," Mary Lou said—she was shouting, standing in the middle of the barn's dirt floor. She kicked the dirt one last time, then—her arms swinging like scythes at her sides—she walked out the open south end. Spring, she thought. Drive a person plumb to madness, and it was a damned short drive.

Mary Lou walked to the John Deere, grabbed a heavy-gauge iron chain with both hands near its end. She pulled on the chain and it clanked off the tractor onto the ground. She dragged the end of the chain to the barn, wrapped it around the corner post, stuck a U-bolt through two links to tie it. She walked back to the tractor and tied the chain's other end to a hitch at the rear.

"Shut up, Buck," she called to the barking dog, still tied to the wheelbarrow. She stopped, picked up a rock, and chucked it in Buck's direction. The dog dropped to the ground, its head on its front paws. "It's all right, Buck," she said. "It won't be long now."

She climbed into the tractor's iron seat and turned the key in the ignition, cranking the motor until it caught. She pulled the throttle as she let out the clutch. The tractor, old but still powerful, pulled the barn's corner post loose. As Mary Lou kept the tractor heading straight another twenty yards, the barn collapsed and lay flat. Buck, yelping and whining, struggled to get free of the rope.

"Tell it adios, Buck," Mary Lou said. "I told that damned Chub once, I told him a thousand times, I'm sick of looking at that piece-of-shit barn. My granddaddy built it, my daddy used it, took good care of it, and me and you, Chub, well …"

Mary Lou stopped talking, turned off the tractor's engine, and sat motionless in the seat.

"I have been on this pitiful place for way too long," she said, speaking to herself again, a practice she had taken up when she and Chub stopped talking. I was born here and I was a girl here, she thought. I don't know anymore what the hell I am.

***

As she stared to the west across the flattest geography in Texas, Mary Lou could see weather building. She'd heard the report that morning. A storm was on its way, and in that country and at that time of year, a storm did not mean rain. In spring, storm references in West Texas promised hellfire and brimstone. Years without rainfall or irrigation to dampen unbroken fields meant sand—as fine as calibrated grains in an hourglass—blasting unimpeded across the land. Pushed by winds upwards of sixty miles an hour, miniscule shards would strike like tiny darts from God's blowgun. As she sat there on the tractor, Mary Lou noticed occasional tufts of dust spiral up from the earth and spin away, dozens of little surprises, rising like bubbles popping to the surface of a tar pit—hints of more implacable astonishments to come. Mary Lou nodded her head.

"Let her blow," she said.

She climbed down from the tractor, took a rag from beneath the seat, tied it to a piece of baling wire, and rammed it into the tractor's gas tank. She pulled the contraption out of the tank, and pushed it back in, the soaked end left dangling. Buck's food bowl caught in a tumbleweed bounded past as Mary Lou, on the lee side of the weathered old house, lit an oil smudge they'd used back when they had cows to keep mosquitoes away during calving time. She put the smoldering smudge—a simple match would never stay lit in a high wind—in a battered metal cooler and loosely closed the lid. She put the cooler on the ground near the tractor, then walked briskly back to the house, smiling and laughing.

The wind plastered the screen door against the side of the house and she yanked it open. Chub was right where she'd left him, out cold, his tiny feet splayed wide on the kitchen's flower-patterned linoleum floor, strapped with duct tape to the chair.

Mary Lou stood, her hands on her hips, looking down at her husband. She opened a drawer in the counter, took out a knife and sliced the tape. She put the knife back in the drawer, walked to the old Chambers stove— connected by heavy-duty plastic pipe to the long propane tank beside the house—and picked up the greasy cast-iron frying pan. She filled the pan with water at the sink, and poured all of it over Chub's bleeding head.

She waited, watching, as he took a deep breath, rolled his head slowly on his neck, grimacing, his eyes closed. He groaned and raised his right hand to his face. He blinked his eyes, tried to open them. Chub, his red hair now graying at the temples, dressed as always in blue mechanic's overalls. He groaned again.

Mary Lou said, "We got a big storm coming, be here before your bedtime." She poked her husband in the chest with her finger, her face no more than two inches from his. "It's gonna blow a lot of old stuff far, far away, Chub. A lot of stuff, Chub. Gonna blow it away."

Chub's body was limp on the chair. His head fell forward on his chest then lolled to one side. His arms, unusually long for a man his size, dangled loosely and the backs of his hands rested like rags on the floor. He slowly raised his head and opened one eye. He blinked around the room.

"Remember how you used to hunker down, helpless in the wind?" Mary Lou said, raising the frying pan in her right hand, spitting into the palm of her left. "Couldn't stand it then, can't stand it now, so you just let it all go to hell. And me, too, didn't you, Chub? Kissed me good-bye right along with the rest of it."

Mary Lou spread her legs a little wider and whacked Chub with the frying pan. Chub's forehead split open. Blood ran through his beard, darkened his blue work shirt, and dripped to the floor. His body slipped to the left, dragging the chair with him to the floor.

As Mary Lou put the pan back on the stove, a section of the barn's tin roof blew past the kitchen window. She heard the dog barking and howling, still held by the weight of the wheelbarrow. She stood silently, looking out the window while the wind picked up speed. She heard the five-gallon bucket she left standing beneath the eve of the house rattle off down the fence line. She leaned on her hands against the counter and wept.

"Dear God in Heaven," she said, speaking just above a whisper. She wiped her eyes on her sleeve then felt Chub's hand, down low, on her right ankle.

Mary Lou kicked backwards at him. She held onto the cabinet as she stomped at his head with her left foot. Chub dropped his hand. He lay still on the floor.

Mary Lou stood, looking down at him. She breathed deep, took his legs by the ankles, and dragged him out the door and through the windswept dirt yard. Another sheet of tin blew by and ricocheted off the side of the house.

Blowing dirt struck her face as Mary Lou dragged her husband to the back of the John Deere, squatted, wrapped her long arms around his waist, took a deep breath and, grunting like an Olympian in the dead lift event, raised him high enough to hook the straps of his overalls over the back of the seat. Holding her arm in front of her face to block sand from her eyes, Mary Lou climbed onto the tractor, started it, and turned it to face her ancestors' homestead. She pulled the throttle to low, and jumped to the ground. She watched from her hands and knees as the tractor moved slowly toward the house.

Mary Lou got to her feet. She took the hot smudge from the cooler and walked swiftly, holding onto the tractor as she held the smudge to the gasoline-soaked cloth, flapping wildly from the mouth of the tractor's gas tank. The cloth immediately flared, and Mary Lou ran from the tractor. The timing was accurate, like the old pick-and-roll the girls used to run on the basketball court. The tractor and then the propane tank exploded just as the John Deere barged through the back door.

The house, in which Mary Lou's mother and two aunts had been born, in which Mary Lou had been raised and loved and from which she had been sent away with high hopes into the world, simply went off like a bomb. Standing near the rubble of the barn, her arms shielding her face from the heat of the blaze, Mary Lou saw Chub's body, dangling from the tractor seat, flaming, like an ornament on a Christmas tree.

***

As Mary Lou untied the rope from Buck's neck, she shook her left hand and cursed when the troublesome pinkie finger, which stuck out at a right angle, caught on the dog's collar. Another damned battle scar, she thought, putting the finger to her mouth. In a fit of rage one Thanksgiving, Chub had tried to lock her in the bathroom. Mary Lou threw her hand out to catch the door, and the pinkie was smashed against the jamb. An accident. That's how Chub had explained it. He said it didn't mean a thing.

Mary Lou watched as Buck, free of the wheelbarrow, ran back and forth between the house and the barn, barking, then sitting and whining, then running again. She walked, head down against the wind, dragging the short piece of rope behind her, to a stack of old boards and junk Chub had piled as high as his head. She pitched the piece of rope on the pile. It caught in the tattered fringe of net that remained on the steel basketball goal Chub had pushed over with the backhoe before the oil pan gasket wore out and the motor threw a rod. Mary Lou had fired thousands of shots at that goal, when she was growing up. It took her father almost a week to turn a part of the backyard into a court on which Mary Lou could play. Chub said it was a nuisance, always in the way.

"Just forget about it," he said. "All that's over and done with."

The house was burning three miles from the nearest road. The blaze was not substantial—a kitchen, a small front room, bedroom and bath— and Mary Lou was not worried. The chances were less than unlikely that it would be seen through the blowing dirt and debris. Only murderous house- wives would be outside on so miserable a day, Mary Lou thought, and she smiled and shook her head.

She pulled a kerchief from her pocket, tied it around her face, and walked a hundred yards to the little family graveyard. Her own grandfather, her mother's father, had told her stories about uncles and great-aunts, cous- ins, all buried there—"still together now," he'd say, "a family, the way the Good Lord meant us to be." Her grandfather had his own place in the little cemetery, beside his wife and their son, who would have been Mary Lou's great-uncle Ben had he lived. But he died before he was two when a giant plow horse named Sam suffered a heart attack and fell, smashing the life out of Mary Lou's great-uncle and breaking her great-great-grandmother's back. She was holding the baby in her arms, letting him pat Sam, the old horse. Another family story Chub didn't want to hear.

"All that old stuff? Shit, ain't nothing about it special," he'd said. "Just keep it to your own self." And Mary Lou did not mention it again, but nei- ther did she forget.

The family cemetery, filled with so many memories, was not neglected. Mary Lou regularly tended it, even after Chub scraped the mounds and headstones away with the front bucket on that same backhoe. Another ac- cident.

"Just got away from me," he said. "Happened in an instant. Well, what the hell? Won't nobody know the difference."

Mary Lou folded her arms across her large breasts and in her mind she shaped one last apology. "I'm sorry, so sorry" were the words she had so often spoken. If she did more than think the words this time, the sound was lost in the wind.

***

She walked back toward the house. Just over an hour had passed, and the fire had diminished to hardly more than an intermittent flicker. The storm, however, continued to rage as evening approached and the sky darkened. She opened the door of the cab-over camper on the back of the pickup truck and climbed inside. Earlier that day, she had packed a small bag with essentials and a larger duffel with her clothes—a dress, a clean pair of Levi's, socks and underwear, a pair of nice boots—and loaded them into the camper.

Crouching beneath the low ceiling, she turned when she heard Buck whining at the camper's back step. Mary Lou clapped her hands and called to the dog.

"Come on in here, puppy," she said. "Wasn't any of it to do with you."

Buck clambered into the camper and she patted him, rubbed his head and his ears.

The dog lay down, and Mary Lou smiled.

A Matter of Life and Death, Seemingly

Patrick Hannon

One chilly Friday evening in the winter of 1976, Ann Pagenheart, a co-worker of mine at McDonald's, stood by my side in a line outside the Chabot Theatre on Castro Valley Boulevard in my hometown. We were there to see Arthur Hiller's Silver Streak, a light romantic comedy—a safe bet. Earlier in the week I had finally gotten the nerve to ask Ann out on a date, even though she was a girl clearly out of my league. I knew it. JP Penrod, Babe Willis, and Bob "Boober" Gerstenberger—my posse since kindergarten—knew it. My four older brothers knew it. I came into the world a puny three pounds-fourteen ounces and was quickly splashed with baptismal waters by Father Stack. Apparently no one had expected me to live. The youngest of five pugilistic brothers, I was lucky to make it to age sixteen. So now I was a puny sixteen-year old kid with big ears and freckles and a cracked voice. Before I died, I wanted to say I had gone out on a date with Ann Pagenheart. I wanted to say that I had kissed Ann Pagenheart without having to lie about it later. I didn't think it was too much to ask.

As I observed her from the corner of my eye that evening as we stood in the cold night, it was clear that by any reasonable standard, Ann was stunningly gorgeous—classic Northern Californian, fresh, natural; viz., the standard for feminine beauty anywhere, circa 1976. Her straight dark brown hair, luscious, and parted elegantly down the middle a la Jaclyn Smith of Charlie's Angel's fame, lay resplendent on her slight shoulders. I had fantasized every day about running my fingers through that hair. Everything about her face pleased me: her soft blue eyes with a tasteful hint of mascara and eye shadow for accent; her cute button nose, her dimples. And those lips. I could have written a treatise on those satin lips. They kept me from a sound sleep in those days. Sometimes I would watch her when we were working the same shift at McDonald's. I'd be at the grill flipping burgers and she would be taking an order at the front counter a few yards away, and I would home in on those lips, hoping beyond hope that she would lick them.

Yes, it was a miracle. That's the only way I can explain how it was that I was standing next to Ann Pagenheart that night.

A week earlier, as I held the receiver in my hand and slowly dialed her number on the rotary phone on our kitchen wall, my heart thumped wildly in my chest. I imagined myself as one of those Acapulco cliff divers before he leaped. I could handle the rejection. I was no idiot: my expectations were firmly grounded in reality. But what if she said yes? What would I do then? Vertigo set in.

"Hello?" she said.

"Hello, is Ann Pagenheart there?" I said. Why I said her last name is a mystery to me even to this day.

"This is she." Score ten big points for Ann Pagenheart. She knew how to speak grammatically.

"HiAnnthisisPatHannonPatHannonfromMcDonaldsandIwaswonderingifyouwouldliketogoouttoa moviewithmeFridaynight?" There was a pause of five seconds or so.

"Which movie?"

"Silver Streak." I was about ready to pass out. She didn't say anything for maybe five more seconds.

"Okay."

"Okay?"

"Okaaay, " she said as if I were hard of hearing.

"I'll pick you up at 7?"

"Okay."

Now on a cool Friday evening I stood next to Ann outside the theatre dressed in my dark brown Angel Flight bell bottomed three-piece suit and a lime-green polyester shirt with fashionably wide lapels and the two top buttons unfastened, very *dans le vent*. Even with my two-inch platform shoes, I stood five feet two and three quarter inches tall. Ann wore tight Levi's that coyly hugged her waist and a halter-top that exposed her delicate shoulders. She towered over me by at least five inches, but I didn't care. She was mine for two hours. If I was lucky, maybe three.

We had been in line for around ten minutes before we finally reached the box office, so I had exhausted all the conversation prompts I had carefully compiled the day before and committed to memory. We were reduced to talking about our pets. My family had a surly, fourteen-year-old, incontinent Chihuahua named Bambi that Grandma Hannon had bequeathed to my mother—who loathed it. Ann had a Bassett Hound named Boozer.

"Do you smoke pot?" Ann said at the exact moment Mr. Toller in the box office came into full view. Mr. Toller and his wife built the theatre in the '50's and had run it ever since. Perched behind the tiny glass-encased booth to the right of the entrance to the theatre, Mr. Toller raised his eyebrows, and his eyes behind his thick black-rimmed glasses sort of bugged out. He knew my family well. My dad's law office was a block away. Sometime in the early sixties, my dad had done some legal work for Mr. Toller and Mr. Toller suggested that in lieu of monetary compensation, any of my father's nine kids could come to the movies at his theatre for free, an offer I suspect he lived to regret. In 1968 I saw Chitty Chitty Bang Bang twenty-one times, a personal best.

"Two tickets, please," I said to Mr. Toller in my most polite voice.

"Five dollars," Mr. Toller said. He was making me pay for both tickets.

"Sometimes I smoke pot," Ann said matter-of-factly, "right before I take a big exam. I find it really helps." She flipped her hair back and giggled. "You should try it."

Was she high? Directly above the entrance to the big tan box of a theatre was a two-sided, brightly lit art-deco marquee. I imagined large black letters on both sides of that marquee spelling out my predicament that evening. On one side it read, "I, PAT HANNON, AM ON A DATE WITH ANN PAGENHEART!" On the other it simply said, "HELP ME."

I gave Mr. Toller a five-dollar bill, and he slid two ticket stubs through the curved small opening where the glass met the small counter; he shook his head slowly in disgust or disappointment, I wasn't sure which, as he placed the bill in the cash register. He seemed to shut the cash drawer with a condemnatory shove. I took my stub and placed it in the inside pocket of my suit jacket and handed the other to Ann. Together we walked into the theatre.

The lobby of the Chabot Theatre was ridiculously small and it seemed to shrink when Ann and I entered it. Roly-poly Mrs. Toller in her ridiculously blonde beehive hairdo sat behind the concession counter in an old swivel chair that squeaked every time she shifted her girth so she could reach the popcorn machine or draw sodas from the fountain behind her without getting up. A dozen or so patrons filled the lobby. Peering over their shoulders, she took note of Ann and then me as we took our place in line. She gave me a look. Are you insane? She seemed to be asking me. Do you know what you are doing? I looked away. The walls of the lobby were school-bus yellow brick and supported a number of thin gold-rimmed glass display cases with posters of upcoming films. Durable crimson red-colored carpet covered the floor. It lent the place a regal air it really didn't deserve. Stale popcorn and straw wrappers and Jujubes and gummy bears littered the lobby. The one light fixture in the foyer, a large opaque-white globe that descended from the geographical center of the lobby, was filthy. I noticed thirty or so fly carcasses collected at its curved bottom. I looked up at Ann. She was staring straight ahead. I began to sweat. I had no business being there with Ann and her perfect ear lobes each punctuated with a tiny hole. Omigod, I thought. She's not wearing earrings. Our date did not warrant accessorizing of any kind apparently. When she looked away I quickly sniffed one of my armpits.

***

Though my dad—a potato farmer's son—was a lawyer and my mom came from good, decent working class Oakland stock, I knew instinctively that my people were members of the *hoi polloi*; we were borderline northern California hillbilly. The very shirt I was wearing that night had been my brother Greg's, and before him, for a short while, my brother Mike's. The brown socks I wore that night were my sister Sally's. But I have to plead desperation on that count. I had no brown socks and I was determined to be color-coordinated that night and those socks matched perfectly with my Angel Flight slacks.

Ann Pagenheart, on the other hand, hung out with the Castro Valley Swim Club Coppertone nouveau riche. She lived off Calaveras Canyon Road where people owned thoroughbreds and had cellars stocked with wines whose names began with Chateau; people who employed fastidious maids in their houses with wrought iron gates and outdoor intercom and video systems to keep out the riff-raff. I lived on Knoll Way, a street that sounds bucolic but instead sadly hugs the border separating the decent folk in Castro Valley from the riff-raff in Hayward. Kids from the riff-raff side regularly threw rocks from their demeaning hovels below us into our green-algaed, tadpole-infested swimming pool.

After the movie I would take Ann to my home to meet the parents. They had insisted on it and made it a condition for my using the family car that night. My brothers and sisters of course would be hanging around in a conspicuous and utterly embarrassing fashion. Julie, the youngest at 11, would probably jump on Ann's lap, that is, if Ann dared to sit on our plastic-covered couch. Greg and Jack would probably squeeze in and sit on either side of her and say howdy-do, you sure are a cute one; and while Dad would refrain from burping and Mom from cussing, they would still be Mom and Dad smiling in that totally helpless and exposed way that parents sometimes do when they realize their children aren't really children anymore but fledgling grownups; that is, in a completely mortifying sort of way. Ann would take a good look at my home and its inhabitants, I thought as I stood there in Chabot's crowded lobby, and that would be the end of it.

Our home had a look and feel that actually scandalized me as a boy. Framed pictures tilted and windows bore cracks and chairs wobbled and green deep shag carpet harbored a thousand fleas in my home. I was never around to see the judges and lawyers and their wives who spent the occasional Saturday afternoon or evening with my parents in their natural habitat. I was never around after the eating and drinking and laughing and sighing, as they walked to their cars in slow, satisfied ambles. It would be much later before I realized that dust and detritus and dirty dishes abound in enviably happy places too. I was born into a tribe that eschewed décor and fidgeted around fancy things and felt deep down more at home in the muck than in a pristine museum.

I was slow in those days to appreciate the gift of lived-in places. I pause uneasily now as I recall the horror I often felt as a child when I brought friends home to play. I took note of the expressions on their faces when they saw my mother in her worn gingham dress and pink slippers at noon raking the living room shag carpet while humming along with Herb Alpert and the Tijuana Brass, a cigarette dangling remarkably from her lips. I took alarming note of my friends as they inspected the doors to our bedrooms— all of them pock-marked and punctured by fists and hurled objects. I gauged their discomfort as they beheld one of my brothers—stripped to his tighty whiteys—walking languidly from his bedroom to the bathroom scratching his belly. How could I have mistaken awe and wonder for pity and disgust? A few years ago I bumped into an old friend, Matt—whose family lived in a mansion with a tennis court and a swimming pool and a live-in maid on tony Massachusetts Avenue—and he told me how lucky he thought I was. "Hannon," he said, "I loved coming to your house. I could breathe there."

But I was 16-years old then and swayed by voices that said a life worth living came with a beautiful woman on your arm, fancy duds on your bones, a beautiful showcase of a home and a country club-coiffed family. I was so Bobby Brady slash Danny Partridge then and not who I really wanted to be: an older Jody from A Family Affair with a butler named French and a panoramic view of Central Park from my Manhattan apartment.

Judging from the manicured front lawn and the freshly painted house and the tasteful, unbroken furniture on display through the living room window—which I took note of when I pulled up to Ann's house earlier that night in the dented '67 Dodge Dart that Dad had bought us kids from a police auction for $250 bucks—I knew that taking Ann to a movie at Chabot Theatre instead of the state-of-the-art multiplex near Southland Mall was going to be a stretch. Only now do I realize that maybe I was easing her into my life, that Ann would come to know me, but only slowly and in small bits and pieces. Anything more would scare her off.

***

The full lobby bustled and buzzed with anticipation when we entered. The usual suspects breathed in air, suffused with popcorn butter molecules. Crazy, bald-headed Tony—who rode his Huffy bike every day down the boulevard, rain or shine, collecting aluminum cans—was rummaging through the garbage can. Mr. Medioti in his fedora stood next to Mrs. Medioti in her faux chinchilla shoulder wrap. They appeared unhappy at having to stoop to a farcical comedy. J.P., Babe, and Boober observed me as I guided Ann Pagenheart closer to the concession counter, and it felt good for once to be observed. A woman tried to squeeze by me on her way to the bathroom, and I inadvertently brushed up against Ann. My hand made gentle contact with her thigh. I nearly fainted. A minute later I got so close to Ann that my nose actually touched her hair as it rested on her left shoulder. I breathed in deeply and smelled her sweet perfume. (She was wearing perfume! Yes!) I nearly fainted. Ann seemed oblivious to the tingling in my fingers, the goose bumps on my arms, the shiver down my spine. It was sufficient for the moment that she did not turn up her nose and suggest that we leave.

It took us ten minutes to get to the front of the line. I had nothing more to say. Ann passionately extolled the virtues of recreational marijuana use, and I played in my mind the conversation I would be having with my father the next day in his law office after he got the phone call from Mr. Toller. Mrs. Toller knew my order by heart: a box of Flicks (the best chocolate morsels Ghirardelli ever confected) and a large Coke, extra ice. Ann ordered a large Tab. I paid in cash and handed Ann her soda. We proceeded past the heavy purple drapes that separated the lobby from the auditorium and entered the theatre proper.

My older brother Greg had told me earlier that if I wanted to neck, the balcony was the place to go. He winked when he said it, which now feels a little creepy but then seemed almost dangerous. I knew what he was getting at. The Chabot Theatre balcony was where every teenager in town snuck up to if they planned to make out. Aware of this, Mrs. Toller regularly ferreted teenagers out of her balcony with a flashlight, a stern look, and curt reminder that the balcony was for adults only.

With Ann at my side now, I gave the balcony to my left a passing glance as we emerged from the short passageway that brought us to the theatre seats and breathed a sigh of relief when I noticed all fifty or so seats pretty much occupied. The thought of being 86ed from the balcony that night was too much to bear. I gave a wide sweep of the lower seating area, divided as it was into three sections. The largest one in the middle accommodated approximately one hundred and fifty seats and the two sections hugging the walls maybe sixty each. Ann and I walked down the aisle on the right that sloped gracefully toward the screen now hidden behind a huge green and gold-striped curtain. I looked to the left and then to the right. As we passed row after row it became clear that there were no seats available. Once or twice I enquired, but the empty ones were spoken for. Ann and I reached the last row, the one closest to the screen, and found two together.

We flipped the thinly upholstered seats down, and as we settled ourselves in, the springs moaned and the joints creaked, five feet from the screen. I looked over at Ann and rendered an apologetic smile. She looked straight ahead and sipped her soda through her straw. We slid down our seats so our heads rested against the top of the seats and at an angle that allowed us to see as best we could the movie that would momentarily begin. Her right arm rested on our shared armrest. Her delicate porcelain hand dangled off the edge.

This is what I imagined:

When the darkness came I would place my left arm against hers on the armrest and then naturally take hold of Ann's hand. After a while I would raise my arm and slide it between her seat and her shoulders. In the dark I would move my body closer to her body so my arm around her shoulders could slowly move down and touch the merest edge of her left breast. I would go no further. Ann would look over to me and smile. She would lean her head against my neck and breathe deeply. She would let me kiss her hair. After the movie We would go for an ice cream at Loard's Ice Cream Shop in the Village and under bold fluorescent lights and behind large paned-glass windows we'd split a hot fudge sundae for all the world to see. Afterward we would drive to Lake Chabot at the edge of town and sit by the docks and hold hands again. In the moonlight, she would let me kiss her. A school of fish, Mr. Limpet-style, would poke their heads up from beneath the water and smile at us. I would take the long way to her home and walk her to her front door gentlemanlike, and under the soft canopy of porch light I'd press my body against hers gently and kiss her on the cheek and she would blush and slay me. She would eventually meet my parents and find them refreshing. She would tell me that she absolutely adored my family and would in time have many dinners at my house and grow to love meat loaf and mashed potatoes and green beans and powdered milk. J.P., Babe, and Boober would be ape-shit jealous and this would please me. Ann and I would marry and have five children and a home that had that lived-in texture to it. Our friends would be able to breathe in our home.

***

The lights dimmed and the large curtains in front of us parted slowly and the audience tittered and lightly applauded. In the now darkened theatre, I very slowly maneuvered my left hand from my lap to where Ann's hand rested. I touched the palm of her hand with the sensitivity of a feather and a longing that only a sixteen-year-old boy can speak of with any real authority. Without looking over, she moved her hand away deliberately and placed it securely on her lap.

***

I went with some friends a week or so later to see Silver Streak again, not for any reason remotely masochistic. I simply did not remember the movie the first time I saw it, for obvious reasons. But then again, seeing the movie that second time now seems like a triumphant gesture, a kind of elegant flipping of the bird to the painful vicissitudes of male teenage life, its built-in angst and fears. I won't lie and say I wasn't completely and totally and absolutely crushed that night. I was. Sometimes I wonder where Ann Pagenheart is now. I hold no grudges. But I won't sit here and tell you that the 114 minutes I spent in that front row next to Ann Pagenheart didn't feel like 114 years because they did. And I certainly won't tell you that I didn't cry a little that night when I was alone in bed while my brothers snored around me. No, I won't lie. What I will tell you is that I got over it. Ann Pagenheart was sexy and smart and a little dangerous and achingly unfathomable and deeply mysterious to me back then. She was everything my 16-year-old heart could have hoped for. Still, she wasn't mine. I'm glad I was Icarus-crazy, though, to think that maybe, if I'd been a little taller, she could have been.

Late August Night

Caitlin Diehl

The heat drove me from my bed
to the kitchen to eat
pineapple
straight from the bowl
each bite so juicy
yellow and cold
to reflect on a future
not-so-distant night
when the cancer will eat
through the heart of our once-whole life
leaving me frozen
alone and suddenly old.

Silence and Me
Dan Encarnacion

silence leans
against a tree
covers its eyes
with meaty hands
I run laughing
below barren branches
hearing myself
kick cantankerous leaves
silence counts

up to a hundred
scrambles and scurries
smell me
pounces
plants
a kiss thick
tongue tight seal
wrestle us
down

press against
my breast
I pull out
my pen
reach and scrawl
a four letter word
on its back
silence can not
bind my hands

—hush

Aposiopesis
Dan Encarnacion

molasses tar
ride jaundice
lights red veins
rolling red vines
thru sweat
on the window
what's the taste of red
what's the taste of red
you're some
where where
I can't touch
your cuticle
the moon
lays a hoary
laundry line
wind
the pulley
on the corner
of the house
creaks
I'll do a load
in the morning
before I go
to bed

Fidelity
Rick Stoddart

Fidelity in all quarters
without dynamics
without illumination
just a rock and a fist
pounding into the soft insides
bruising a most purple-brown
the science of it all.
Batting eyelashes
become the method
deconstructing every hypothesis
despite the grimaces and groans
as the cars go by
and by and
in no particular order, rearranging
our cells through dampened fumes
in darkness and flesh.
Consistency becomes the
deflated
currency
we all stuff under our pillows –
so much, the better.

A Table in Space
Amy Miller

I love my big,
loud friend
who mauls waiters
and always orders
the jumbo beer,
anything named "fat" or "ass,"
who stabs his steak
with no remorse
for yesterday's slaughter,
for nitrates and fat
rushing to the demolition
of his heart.
I love the way
I sometimes think
of turning down
the volume knob
under his shirt,
the big one in the middle
among the dials for dirty jokes,
the switch
for sudden tenderness,
the gauge
with this father's death
at the red end
where the needle pins.
The way the evening
seems like a month,
the way the roof
leans over him,
listening for his praise—
this is why I stay,
his pool of gravity
bending the table,
bottles docked
next to the spaceships

of our bodies, my ears
turning their great dishes
toward him,
sifting out of the night
his one strong signal.

Fence

Dan Encarnacion

We write our names in the snow
Under aegis of our forsaken lot:
You and I—dueling little boys,
Your Errol Flynn to my . . . O
Who could compare? Your script

Twines with mine and broken ribs
Of gust-busted umbrellas catch.
One juncture of your lips lifts
Into smile and your eyes sear.

Tell me what my face is doing.
If it manages anything at all. You yank
Your gentleman's umbrella from my snare,
Grab my dimestore defect and stab their

Filials into the frozen white drifts
To end-stop our rococo scrawl.
You run off after your smile completes
And sells me your symptoms of joy.

Five Fab Camfire Stories

Through the Window
Grahame Watt

I spent my final year as a Ph.D. candidate in England, sitting in a pub in west London called The Level Crossing. It was one of those classic English pubs that had been around so long that the building itself was a historical monument. The beer was hand-pumped out of ancient oak casks by a crotchety, mostly-blind man stuck in the Blitz. The food was served on thick wood blocks with massive potato wedges or in deep clay bowls tempered by countless portions of rich, steaming stew. On Saturdays, the pub filled with people watching West Ham play while telling bad jokes and draining ale by the pint. Most days, I sat in my seat by the window, drinking tea and working on my dissertation. Emma, the waitress, kept my cup filled and always had a smile and some gentle humor for me. Her father was far less friendly, or maybe just protective. Either way, I got no smiles or pain-less mockery from him, just unintelligible growls and repeated reminders to keep my feet away from the window. The old man didn't so much as glance in my direction; I think he only responds to "ale" and its synonyms.

I don't think I would've spent as much time in the Level Crossing if it weren't for that window. Fifteen feet across, it consisted of sixty panes of glass, all frosted with age. The window bowed out, allowing an unobstruct-ed view of the train station below. Thanks to the relative quiet of modern, high speed trains, the pub was spared most of the rumble of diesel engines and squeal of brakes, leaving me to watch the churning masses of people coming and going in peace.

When I didn't have work to do, or when I just needed a break, I picked people out of the crowd and invented lives for them. For instance, there was the blond woman who always wore massive black sunglasses like they do in Hollywood. She was so determined to make it as an actress that she had already started behaving like a diva, dressing only in expensive designer fashions and throwing tantrums whenever her poor father forgot to evenly dust her French toast with organic nutmeg. She was so convinced that her big break was just days away that she refused to address her ailing finances and her massive credit card debt, no matter how often the bill collectors called her.

Then there was the Pakistani with the blue turban who changed trains here, commuting into London from some village out past Reading. At home he suffered nervous looks from neighbors whose xenophobia is softened only by fond memories of Aladdin. His first train pulled in two platforms away from his waiting connection, and he was always ten steps too slow to make it. It happened every day, but he never once so much as jogged in an attempt to save himself fifteen minutes. He was a man of tremendous character, a man who holds his dignity in the highest esteem. I think that he secretly enjoyed the accidental discrimination of the timetable, a warm-up snub before a long day of subtle ostracism.

When business was slow and she finished her chores, Emma often joined me at my table. Normally, I was working on my dissertation— "Theoretical and Empirical Studies on High Speed Transit and Service Sector Output"—so she sipped a glass of lemonade and did the cross-word while I played with data sets. Other times, I let my computer crunch numbers and we talked. Usually she ranted about being ignored by whoever she happened to be dating at the time. She was not a gifted storyteller; her outrage was too shrill, her frustration too tragic, and it often seemed like my reaction was more important to her than her ire. I never met any of these people, not Aaron with the perfect smile, nor Ian with the deep blue eyes, nor Paul the French exchange student. When she ran out of horror stories, I shared some of my thoughts on the people down below. Like the bloated, grinning mechanic who stood on the third platform, ignoring the crumbs cascading down his coveralls from whatever strange sandwich he was always eating. When his train pulled in, he tossed whatever was left of his meal in the direction of the bin and saunters aboard. He always missed, and the sandwich went bouncing down the platform, lunch meat sailing off in all directions. Sometimes I wanted to march down there, pull him off the train, and make him throw his food away. Emma laughed when I told her about his habits.

"You're ridiculous," she said.

"It's not that funny."

"It is a bit. You get all riled up about a fat man on a train station."

"Maybe a little."

"Well, anyway, why don't you go down there and talk with him?"

"It goes against the rules."

"You have rules?"

"Sure. Well, one rule."

"Which is?"

"Don't interfere."

Emma got up, smoothed out her black apron, and collected the empty bowl and beer glass from my table. She flicked a straight brown bang out of her face with her free hand.

"Of course not. They're just stories."

"Right." The murmured agreement floated around in my head. They're just stories.

***

It was the sundress that first caught my eye. A white, satin number devoid of frills, it was the dress of the dream girl, the woman that had grown up unaware of the hero's silent infatuation. She picked her way through the mass of people on Platform Two, her slow careful movements out of place amongst the mad rush of commuters. I sipped my tea and watched as she sat on the bench at the end of the platform, crossing her legs and folding her hands in her lap. Then my laptop beeped, demanding my attention. I brought up my buggy program and returned to work, pushing the woman out of my mind.

It took me an hour or so to figure out what the problem was with my code, and another four to sort it out. The lunch rush had come and gone; so rather than bother the cook for food I went out and bought a curry, which I ate at a bench across the street from the police station. Exotic odors mixed with the crisp smell of fallen leaves, and I couldn't help but smile, both at the weather and at the drunken man a pair of constables half-led, half-dragged into the station. He hiccuped a few times, face flushed with alcohol, and then stumbled through the doors. If his grin was any indication this wasn't the first time he had been picked up, and it wasn't going to be the last. Still, I couldn't help but admire his cheerfulness as I walked back to the Level Crossing.

I returned to my spot to find Emma in my seat, playing Minesweeper on my computer, her feet on the sill. I sat across from her, taking a sip from the beer that she had left me.

"I've never understood what people see in this game," she said, not looking up from the screen.

"So why are you playing it?"

"I'm bored."

"Exactly. That's why people play it."

She looked up at me.

"So how come you don't?"

"I don't get bored."

"Right. You have the lives of others to keep you entertained."

"You say that like it's my fault and I've never had any luck with other people," she said. "I get impatient, I want in. Instead, they just go about their lives, oblivious to my presence."

"I think you might be missing the point."

"I know you are."

I didn't respond. I could feel her eyes scrutinizing my face and I did my best to keep it blank. Finally, she gave up and slid out of the bench, wiping her hands on her apron.

"I'll let you get back to work"

Emma disappeared into the kitchen, leaving me to ponder her words in silence. I got up and slid back into my usual spot. Pulling my glass across the table, I glanced out the window and then froze at the sight of the woman in white.

***

She hadn't moved from the bench in over six hours. It's as though the Tin Man, on holiday from Oz, had strolled down the platform, decided that the bench looked comfortable, and rusted in place. Every conceivable train to every conceivable location had come and gone dozens of times. She didn't work there; even at this distance I could tell that her pale, smooth face was one that belonged in the top floors of an office building, not amongst the grime and muck of the train station. A constable loitered nearby, keeping an eye on the woman. He wasn't suspicious, just curious. He'd never seen anything like it. The woman shoots him a small smile, appreciative of his concern and the constable nodded in acknowledgement before strolling off to deal with a man who had begun proselytizing to a very uncomfortable group of old ladies waiting for the train to Gatwick.

We sat for another hour, she on her bench and me at the window. She wrapped herself in a shawl, and I finished my beer, but otherwise we were still. My laptop beeped a few times, trying to get my attention, and then died with a pathetic squeak. I stuffed it into my bag in annoyance, crumpling a few of my papers in the process. Men just getting off work started streaming in, and the familiar buzz of melded voices began to grow. The ambient noise only intensified my focus and it was not until Emma tapped me on the shoulder that I realized that some of the regulars were watching me with unease.

"What's wrong? You're putting everyone on edge."

I took a breath. "Nothing is wrong."

"Right. Of course it isn't."

"It's not."

Emma said nothing.

"Fine." I sighed. "That woman is still there."

"So what? Can't come up with a plausible explanation?"

"No, I—wait. Yes, actually."

"Is that a problem?"

"No. Maybe. I don't know. What would you wait on a bench for hours on end for?"

She gave me an odd look, wiping her hands off on her apron.

"You want my advice." It wasn't really a question.

"Sure."

"Break your rule."

***

The sun was minutes away from setting by the time I reached the platform, and the day had softened in anticipation. The woman's pale face, framed by jet black hair, glowed faintly in the orange light. She watched me as I approach, and said nothing when I sat next to her. A thousand questions raced through my mind, but I kept quiet. We sat, watching the crowds rush up and down, tired and cranky, just trying to get home to disinterested spouses and ungrateful children.

One train departed, and another arrived. We didn't say anything.

It was a lot noisier down here, in the middle of everything. The diesel-electric trains thumped as they pulled out of the station, and howled as the expresses raced through. Brakes squealed and doors dinged, all set against a background of hundreds of footsteps. It was smellier here too, thanks to overflowing bins and scattered garbage, but for the moment the only aroma I was registering was a curious mix of oil, autumn, and lavender.

The woman gave a quiet, lilting sigh. Her shoulders slumped slightly as the last vestiges of stubborn hope gave way.

"He's not coming."

Her voice was rich and melodic, with a small waver that sounded more like a vibrato than a note of resignation. I said nothing, preferring to drink it all in.

"It was a long shot at best. It's been five years."

She reached down and picked up her purse.

"You know what the worst part is?"

"No." My voice was no more than a throaty whisper.

"I could sit here for days and wait. In fact, I might come back tomorrow and do just that."

"I don't doubt it."

She rubbed her eye with the back of her hand. "When they say she won't wait forever, that doesn't mean she doesn't want to."

"It only means she won't."

The woman nodded, and stood up. She glanced past me and then gave me a small smile.

"It only means she won't."

I watched her walk away, dress flapping in the breeze, no sign of stiffness in her gait. She thanked the constable, got on the escalator up to the bridge, and disappeared into the mob. I could feel a pair of eyes on my back, eyes in the pub that wonder what revelations I am having, but I didn't turn around. For that moment, it was enough to sit in the cool autumn breeze on a dirty platform west of London, while someone else told a story about me.

I Heard You Were Dead
Tim Pfau

Hearing you were dead, I thought I should check
and strolled down the lane to the small house's
door with your name, the one leaking Beatles,
a much longer walk than it used to be.
Just like always, I knocked, knocked and waited,
waited, like always, for you to answer.
I stood, wondering. You're never on time.
But penny-loafer steps start echoing.
Then it opens and there you are, fifteen,
-wild-curled hair disciplined into a bun,
-smiling at me, -the hall between classes,
-touching my hand, -laughing, sure you're in love,
-your lips tasting my own forty six years
ago, —your face and your eyes and your back
under a black wind breaker leaving me
dissolving through the same mist you've walked in.
No, I heard you were dead, and I will look
into it further, but you seem to be
right where you were, there in the memory,
back on the lane now so rarely walked down.

The Demise of J.N. Rainey
Michael Snider

The Primeval Rogue

I've lost count of the times I've backpacked the first three and a half miles of the Wild section of the Rogue River Trail to a meadow a little past Whisky Creek. Each time I place my tent on the edge of a small copse so it faces west and overlooks a gently sloping meadow of sedge. Below, the darker green water of the Rogue River ambles slowly, peacefully, along the meadow. About two hundred yards downstream a small rapid, by Rogue standards, chops and churns, giving off pleasant background music. In the quiet of night, stones move in the rapid and pound stationary rocks, thrumming like a huge string bass.

I've camped here every season. I've experienced bone-numbing snow and ice, nearly horizontal torrential rain and fog as dense as soupy cement. Once it was 15 degrees in February. Another time, in August, the temperature peaked at 116. Most visits, though, are an alluring amalgam of cool mornings, hot afternoons and tepid evenings. I came first as a troubled teenager. My last sojourn birthed the decision to retire and now gives rise to this writing.

I always situate the tent close to a large, head-high moss covered chunk of incredibly compressed metamorphic rock geologists say belongs to the Rogue Formation. In bad weather I can stretch a tarp between the trees surrounding the rock. This creates a shelter where I can sit and watch the river while my back rests against the cold, hard edge of antiquity.

There is something boldly prehistoric about the landscape of the Lower Rogue River Canyon, so that when I come here it is like placing one foot outside of time. The pace of life slows and my inner world gradually awakens like day rising from night on another planet. The exposed geology of the Lower Canyon is some of the oldest in the world. The first formations date back to the Triassic period 250 million years ago when fragments of crustal material from other tectonic plates broke away and "sutured" into ours. The enormous scale of heat, pressure, time and violence involved in this process staggers imagination.

Eighty-five million years later, during the Jurassic period, inconceivably huge forces moved again. In our precinct, they grabbed ancient materials from the bottom of the Pacific Ocean, rammed them into the continental plate, slipped beneath, slid for hundreds of miles, and then blasted — albeit, a very slow blast — through the shelf in the area of what is now called the Klamath-Siskiyou Province. As a result, the rocks along the Lower Canyon are actually older than upstream mountains of the south Cascades.

Early visitors to the Rogue River used words like "wild," "primeval," "untamed" and, of course, "rogue" to describe what they felt. All of these aspects are buried in the river's cryptic geological history. Although geologists know these things, other people sense them without science. This is because the savage forces that inhabited the canyon's early history are still present. They are impregnated deep into the canyon's anomalistic personality. Indeed, all of those wild time-defying forces still tremble below the surface of the landscape, teeming with unconscionable power.

During my last trip to Whisky Creek, after about two miles of hiking very rocky, up-and-down terrain, I came to a place where the trail leveled and passed from exposed rock into shade. The woods are formed mostly of live canyon oak, madrona, big leaf maple and a few Douglas fir. Thickets of many kinds of shrubs and flowering plants, including robust poison oak, entangled the trees and blocked the river from view.

But not from sound.

A steady, ominous rumble foretells the coming of Rainey Falls, a place where the river narrows, squeezed tightly between huge rocks, and then drops fifteen to twenty feet in short measure. You might not call this passage a classic waterfall because the water does not cascade vertically, but in its own way is even more impressive. According to the International Scale of River Difficulty used by boaters to judge rapids, Rainey Falls holds a Class 6 rating, which indicates the highest degree of difficulty. This designation is given when a rapid exemplifies extreme conditions involving unpredictability and danger. The consequence of error is so severe rescue may be impossible. As a result, a side channel has been constructed to skirt rafts around the falls.

There is no other place along the Rogue's Wild designation that lives up to the river's appellation better than Rainey Falls. The falls exhibit such feral, beast-like temperament that it can be easily imagined as a rogue animal.

For me, I see a feline of mythic proportion as the river gathers just ahead of the narrows, compacts, lifts slightly and then quivers as though gathering powerful loins. The beast inches forward. The back arches, the fringe of water trembling and eerily lit as though illumined from within. The head tips up and jaws part to disembowel a furious, guttural spew of white froth. The cold-blooded beast leaps into the air for a tiny moment of suspension. Claws gleam like shards of razor sharp glass. Front feet slam down first, back feet second. The soul-splitting implosion of water sucks surrounding air and drags whatever it holds into the roiling cauldron.

From inexhaustible ancient resources, the beast summons forth icy swells of turbulence and tumult over and over.

There is something so fiercely haunting about the motion of the falls, and the tremors it sends crawling through fissures of rock and earth, that some visitors find themselves under a spell. I see them sitting alone on flat spots as close to the water as they dare, knees drawn tight against their chests, arms wrapped around shins, hands interlocked, bodies rocking gently.

I have often asked people what they experience at the falls that makes their visits special. Answers vary, but the one I hear most goes something like this: "The place makes me think outside myself and sense the presence of something bigger." Another variation: "The place is timeless. It makes me realize just how tenuous life is." It is true. Because of its wildly unpredictable power, Rainey Falls tests a person's view of the world like few places.

Life in the Lower Canyon

Early settlers first named the falls Whisky Creek Falls even though the creek is a little more than a mile downstream. Sometime around 1900 a little known miner by the name of J. N. Rainey moved into the Grave Creek area. He tried his hand at both lode and placer mining here and there, working his way slowly downstream until he reached the Rogue River around 1910. He built a small cabin in the flats on the north side of the river and took up fishing, gaffing salmon and steelhead as they worked their way through the falls. He packed his fish to the town of Glendale, situated a good 25 miles to the northeast along what is now the Interstate, where he sold his catch in the town market. He lived and worked alone from this location but was fondly known by his customers in Glendale, as well as neighboring miners and a few hearty fishermen who endured the primitive roads and trails to fish the Wild River below Grave Creek.

On an unspecified date, probably somewhere in the late 1920s, J. N. Rainey was found dead in his cabin. He had been struck on the head with a heavy object. Information about the murder is scant. In 1978, local historian, Kay Atwood, published a book about the history of the Rogue River Canyon entitled, Illahe, The Story of Settlement in the Rogue River Canyon. It is the only definitive history of Canyon life, especially as it relates to gold miners. I obtained my copy from a used bookstore in Grants Pass in 1980.

Atwood devotes a half page of text specifically to J. N. Rainey and then includes a photograph of Rainey fishing with a gaff at the falls. The author says Ivan Billings, the grandson of original canyon settlers, John and Adeline Billings, told her Rainey was found lying in his bed with a rifle in his lap pointed at the door, a cartridge half way into the chamber.

Little more is known, except the government maps were officially changed. According to brief excerpts from Atwood's interview with pioneer Canyon boatman, Glen Wooldridge, the name for the falls was changed to Rainey Falls after the old man's death. The map amendment opened a new story for me. Like the feral powers imbedded within the landscape surrounding Old Man Rainey's arrival and departure, this new story prowled just beneath the surface.

Rainey's violent death must have been big news in the Canyon. People who knew the slightly built man with the thick, droopy white moustache, said Rainey was uncomplicated, a man who kept to his own business. He had no known disputes or enemies and no one could fathom why anyone would pick on an old man like J. N. Rainey, let alone bust his head while he lay in bed. The crime was never solved.

Gold miners carry extra capacity for hope. They endlessly believe they are just one dig away from the bonanza that will make them rich, and that wealth cures everything. The truth, however, is that gold miners are often misfits. Somewhere their stories went badly until they fled to the margins — in this case the Canyon, a place forged by nature to be a haven for wounded people. As a result, miners also know unabated loneliness and the deep burn of disaffection. These attributes blend and lay dormant until one of their kind is treated unfairly. That is when they combust into fierce, compassionate allegiance, especially when the hurt involves the strong taking advantage of the weak.

Atwood devotes a number of pages to the story of Lou Martin, a miner who lived in the Canyon nearly fifty years and occupied cabins at Howard Creek, Rum Creek and, finally, the cabin and mining compound at Whisky Creek. This area is now preserved by the Bureau of Land Management as a popular visitor attraction. All of the places Martin lived were located within proximity of the falls. Rum and Whisky Creeks are a mile downstream, while Howard Creek, his earliest residence, is three miles further. Much of the material about Martin is transcribed from a lengthy interview obtained just before he passed away in 1977. Martin's story is critical to understanding Rainey's story.

Martin lost his wife and his only child, a baby, to the flu epidemic of 1918, and couldn't stand upstate New York where they had lived together. Eventually, driven by melancholy, he sold everything and headed west. In Yuma, Arizona, an old man told Martin he could live free on government land if he was a miner.

"You can be independent," the man said, "and make a living where people will let you be."

Martin made a sharp right-hand turn and headed straight for Oregon, finally landing in Grants Pass. It wasn't long before he heard about gold mining in the Lower Rogue Canyon. He told Atwood he literally felt something call him to the mountains of the Rogue River. It was a place where he could lose himself. He said it was the only remedy for his kind of sadness. He never lived anywhere else.

Loneliness never bothered him, Martin boasted to Atwood, but later confessed he sometimes got down pretty bad during holidays when he was tempted to go to Grants Pass and stay in a hotel. But he knew the town would be full of families, so he found it better to stay put until his melancholy got better. Martin said the other miners who lived in the hills were the same way. All had histories that had to be respected.

Martin said it was the custom to keep tabs on each other, to drop by from time to time for a cup of coffee and the exchange of news. But the real purpose was to make sure everything was alright. The visitor would keep the stay short, maybe an hour at tops, and then take leave. "Always been that way," Atwood quotes Martin. "If we heard something was wrong, we'd go right now; night or day, if he was sick or hurt and you knew it."

Based upon Lou Martin's stoic description of canyon life, it is easy to imagine what happened when the news of Rainey's senseless death reached other miners. Their hermit-like hearts opened and turned to action by an unspoken code. And so, when the idea of renaming Whisky Creek Falls in J. N. Rainey's honor was mentioned, it took off on strong wings.

Although I found no account regarding the renaming of the falls, the name occurs on the U. S. Geological Survey map (USGS) for the Mt. Reuben Quadrant. I know from experience as a land use planner that changing geographical names on USGS maps required significant effort in the 1920s, just as it does now. A formal petition must be prepared justifying the change and then submitted to a special board of the USGS for review and approval. Who went through all this, just to honor Rainey's memory? I can think of no better candidates than Rainey's closest neighbors.

Atwood's book contains three maps identifying the cabins in the area, and gives names of the occupants, men with names like Dutch Henry, Moody Mike, Price Copsey, Montana Rickett, Cy Whiteneck, Joe Utassey, the Sanderson twins, Clifton and Clayton, and, of course, Lou Martin.

Besides Lou Martin, who by disposition and testimony, is a clear choice, there was also Joe Utassey, a Hungarian immigrant, who lived at China Creek in a cabin which he shared with a ring-tailed cat he had coaxed into a pet. The miners called Utassey "Gigolo" because high energy caused him to bounce like a dancer. Red Keller, an off and on canyon resident interviewed by Atwood, described Utassey as "a little bit of a guy who would follow you around just talkin' and talkin' for miles." Keller said you couldn't go near his cabin or Utassey would harass you into sharing a meal. Atwood reports that Rainey planted an apple tree at Utassey's cabin from a small slip he got from a Chinese miner. This small gesture connected the two miners. Perfect.

There were also the Sandersons, Clifton and Clayton, who Martin described as sociable, busy fellows who worked incessantly like ants. "They was good fellows," was Martin's summation. Clifton enjoyed people and loved to roam the canyon hunting and fishing. He also made wine and shared the fruits of his labor freely. Clayton was the organizer, the ramrod for big projects, including a bridge for pack animals that crossed the river about a mile upstream from the falls.

All four of these men lived within one mile of the falls around the time of Rainey's death. Not much to go on, but for my purpose, it is enough. In the custom described by Lou Martin, they would be ready to go to Rainey's aid right now, day or night, even if it might be too late to save the old man's life. They could still bestow a legacy for his name. It was like putting a shiny gold nugget on top of his grave. It was what they did for their own.

How It (May Have) Happened

The four miners overcame their reclusive tendencies for Rainey's sake and formed what might be fairly described as a civic group. They collected signatures up and down the river. Their petition also included just about every fisherman and visitor who wet a line or passed on the roads or trails in the area. When they had what they thought was a respectable number, they walked the roads that led to the small community of Wolf Creek, 12 miles to the northeast. They started early so they could collect more signatures from the residents and miners along the roads. At Wolf Creek, they worked their petition around town and then caught the late train that took them another 20 miles to the county seat in Grants Pass. They created a stir on the train as they told Rainey's story and leveraged signatures from the crew and passengers.

By the time they debarked at the depot on "G" Street, it was almost dark and the county courthouse was closed. They turned on 6th street and walked two blocks to the Del Rogue Hotel. After some back and forth conversation, the clerk agreed to let a single room to all four. After they got their gear stowed, they went out for food and drink and settled on Digger's Tavern across the street.

Gigolo was ecstatic. "Yi-eee! Dis haf to be da place, uh? Dee-gar's? Ha! Ha!" He danced a jig right there on the sidewalk, flapping his hat against his leg. The others humored him but dreaded the long flood of chatter that lay ahead, especially after a few beers.

The next morning the men were up before daylight. Their plan was to present their petition first thing when the courthouse opened, but this still gave them time for a little food and coffee in the hotel café. They sat quietly in one corner passing around tattered scraps of the weekly newspaper, The Rogue River Courier. Luckily, Gigolo was groggy-headed and taciturn for a change, sitting straight in his chair, arms wrapped around his front, storing up steam for the day.

At a quarter to eight the four miners collected their jackets and knapsacks, paid for their meals, and walked briskly north along 6th street until they reached the steps of the courthouse, where they stood waiting for the doors to open. A few minutes later a janitor unlocked the heavy double oak doors and swung one open. He stood to the side, holding the door for the miners. "Looks like we got some early birds here this fine mornin'," he said in a dry tone. "Come on in and git yer worms."

As the miners passed through the doors, Cliff Sanderson was at the end of the line. Without raising his head, he spoke in a quiet, flat voice, "We've already had a dandy breakfast, thank ya."

They went straight to the board of commissioner's office to present their petition. They asked for the Board Chair, Peter Paxton. Clay Sanderson had barely warmed up his spiel when Pete raised a hand like he was stopping traffic. "You boys need to talk to the surveyor. We ain't got no jurisdiction over federal maps and the surveyor don't neither, but he'll know something about what needs ta be done. See him. He's the friendly fellow down the hall thata' way," he said, pointing. "Two doors down. Oughta be in his office by now." He promptly turned and ambled back toward the door to his office, mumbling as he went. "But you never know about that Meecham."

The surveyor sat in a generous office surrounded by glass cases displaying antique transits, compasses, levels and drafting equipment. One particular case, near the door, showed a collection of local minerals that instantly distracted the miners. Ignoring the surveyor, they gathered around the case.

Clay Sanderson spoke. "Well, well, boys. looky here, will ya!" Clay bent low, resting his hands on bowed knees. He put his nose close to the glass, but stopped short with the soft plunk of the brim of his hat bumping the case. "I'll be beat like a dog if that ain't quartz bearing a hefty vein of gold. See it there on the side, twisten' all pretty like ah ribbon. Like ah Christmas ribbon!"

The others gathered next to Clay and formed a line like boys on a sidewalk in front of a window full of toys. Utassey's eyes twinkled and his fleshy cheeks rolled up until they pinched the corners of his eyes. "Dis ah goud rock! I vunt dis ting in me deeg pre-tay soon. Ha! Ha! Dis be goud ting to av for Joe, uh?"

Lou Martin patted Utassey's back. He could feel him trembling with excitement. "You and who else, Gigolo! Maybe ya need to git your ol' hiney down to the clerk's office and file ah claim on this here cabinet before I do!"

"Sorry, boys." The voice broke into the miners' reverie like a handpick carefully pecking an ore sample. "The county already has first claim on that piece of quartz and all of the ore you can see in this place. I can understand your envy, though. You're looking at a mighty fine specimen. Came out of the Benton mine, a piece out of one of the first assays done on the claim."

Clay Sanderson straightened first, putting a hand to the small of his back and grunting. The others followed suit, moving away from the case reluctantly, squinting at the surveyor as if judging another kind of ore.

"I'm Louis Meecham, County Surveyor. I don't believe I've crossed paths with you boys, but I get the idea you're miners." Louis extended a warm, soft hand and they all shook it vigorously, giving first and last names and the names of their claims.

"I've heard your names bantered around here and there. Nothing bad, of course. Just talk." Louis smiled. "Nice to make your acquaintance. I guess you boys would know a lot more about the Benton mine than me."

"Yup, that would be true," Clay replied in a quiet, understated voice that carried a hefty load of implications. The other miners nodded agreement.

Louis smiled again. It was clear the quaint, wiry little fellow with the bowed legs and wide-brimmed hat was the honcho. "I bet you boys could tell some pretty good stories when there's time. What brings you into my humble bailiwick this fine morning?"

Before the miners could answer, Louis added, "But, first, why don't you all come over here and sit at the table." Louis gestured toward a worn oak table with four matching chairs. "I'll get another chair." He went behind his desk and pulled an office chair over to the table. The miners joined him.

"Alright. What kind of business you got?"

Clay dug into a deep jacket pocket and pulled out a roll of papers held together with burlap string. He pulled on the string and it fell into a limp coil on the table.

"Well sir," he said with a bit of introductory flair, as he unrolled the papers and spread them flat on the table. The papers were crumpled, torn and otherwise liberally stained with dirt and spilt coffee. Clay held them straight with bony fingers.

"We've come with a fine idea. You know 'bout ol' Rainey, don't ya? 'Bout how he was kilt in his cabin ah few months back?"

Louis nodded. "Yes, I do. Made some noise here in the courthouse, I can tell you."

Lou Martin broke in. "Somebody bust his head with a shovel. That's what we've been thinkin'. Somethun' heavy fer sure. Ain't nothin' nobody wants ta see. That's the truth. Was a damnable mess!"

"Yes, I know." Louis folded his hands on the table top. "He didn't deserve to die the way he did. No one does. I agree."

"That's the point we're gettin' at," Clay spoke, regaining the podium. "Rainey never done nobody wrong. He was kinda simple, if you know what I mean. He just done what he done, fishin' at the falls, an' sellin' his fish on the cheap. Never gouged nobody. Never fussed nobody. Only sold good fish. Now they say they don't know who done the murder, killing Rainey like he was a poor animal. Only someone as cold as a rattlesnake at dawn could have done it that way." Clay paused and looked down at the papers and smoothed them, his head bobbing slightly.

It was hard for Louis to tell if the miner was experiencing emotion, so he waited for Clay to look up. When he did, Louis nodded for him to continue.

Clay's voice wavered ever so slightly, then cleared. "Louis, we have here a petition to change the name on the falls. We all want 'em ta be Rainey Falls from here on. Ya know, fer the honor of old man Rainey."

Louis Meecham didn't hesitate. He smiled and reached across the table and took the petition. "I know what needs to be done boys," he said in a soft, confident voice. "I'll see the matter through. You have my word. I've done this before. Can't see a problem. But it's up to the Federal folks to make the final decision."

The miners rose together. Each shook Meecham's hand, looked him straight in the eye and spoke grateful words. They never came back to check on the renaming. They knew Meecham's promise was good.

Tiny Eulogies

The name for the falls changed on the official U.S. Geological Survey Map for the Mount Reuben quadrant two years later. Ever since J. N. Rainey's name has been spoken countless times in connection with the falls. Many of those tiny eulogies occurred at the very scene of the crime, while standing next to the falls. It is certain almost none of the speakers knew anything about J. N. Rainey's cruel death.

The beast in the water, however, hears every spoken word despite the deafening din of its groans, as it pounces endlessly.

The Rogue in the Falls

It was the river that rose up in the middle of that one night, the night J. N. Rainey died. It escaped its banks like a snake crawling from its skin, slithering the short distance to J. N. Rainey's front door. It was holding a smoothly rounded ten pound stone in its watery mouth.

The old man heard huge drops landing hard on the wooden steps leading to the cabin door and thought it was a man's boots. He reached for the rifle next to his bed and quickly loaded a shell and waited for a knock.

The steps stopped. Motionless, Rainey listened intently for a long minute but heard nothing more and wondered whether he had dreamed the sounds. Nervously, he called out, "Who's it out there? Ya better talk up! I got ah gun an' I'll damn well use it if I hafta!"

There was a faint squeak from wood moving against leather hinges stiffened by the cold as the door slowly swung open. The gun discharged with a harsh crack and tart whiff of gunpowder. The bullet pierced the water without effect. So it was the second cartridge they found half-way into the gun's chamber, not the first, when the body was discovered.

As it happened, the water, enticed by a dull glim, scooped up the lone cartridge from the cabin floor in a curling, dripping paw. Later, between the rocks, it rolled the shell back and forth in the moonlight, treating the spent cartridge like a rare curiosity, a memento from travel.

By morning's first gray light the water's interest in the brass tube dulled. Released, the empty shell drifted to the gravel at the river's bottom just below the falls, where it slowly jostled back and forth until it disappeared like a tiny salamander burying itself in mud.

The one who found the body made no note of the faint water stains on the wooden steps and cabin floor. Indeed, they were barely visible at the time of discovery, but even if they had been noticed, nothing would have suggested the water's tie to J. N. Rainey's murder.

A Time for Mourning
Robert Bennett

The older waitress let out a noise like a chicken when Stubby, the short, stocky yarder puncher, reached out and pinched her on the ass as she went by the counter with a load of dirty dishes.

It was an old-fashioned diner in a town too small to sustain fast food. We were here for breakfast and three days behind schedule. Then the waitress with the good butt went to Rich and Harley's booth; Paul and I got the skinny one, and there wasn't much of anything to do after that but eat.

We were working a high-lead side for Standard Lumber out of Yoncalla, but the company had farmed us out to an outfit that was developing real estate in northern California. They'd picked up a big piece a' ground down the Klamath River, somewhere around Hayfork, to build a retirement resort, with a golf course and swimming pools and such. So it didn't matter to them folks what logs was worth—the trees was in the way and they wanted to get rid of 'em. It was kind of a weird deal for us, but the management did that from time to time, when things were slow. The log market had been in the toilet for a very long time now.

We'd moved down over the weekend and we was scheduled to start yardin' logs on Monday—at least we figured on getting the tower set up and the lay-out made—but the folks we were workin' for hadn't realized we'd need a landing, so we had to wait while they hired an old D8 dozer from a road crew workin' down along the highway. They needed to punch in a road and make a place for us to work before we could move a muscle.

Hal Young, our boss and hook-tender, told the head real estate guy, "You might just as well leave that ol' Eight up here. Steep as this ground is, we're gonna have to move every two weeks. It'll be all that old Cat can do, to build roads enough to stay ahead of us."

We'd brought an old Seven with us—on a short low-boy that Stubby drives—but she was a tired old girl with a winch on the back—couldn't rip nothin'. Besides, a Seven's too light to build road in this steep, rocky country. We used her to chase around the landing and move the yarder when we had to.

After breakfast, we all piled in the crummy—except for Hal and Stubby; they took Hal's pickup—and headed to the job. Harley Hansen, the riggin' slinger, drove the crummy, and all the way to the landing all he could talk about was the "the ass on that waitress" back at the diner. "Whoo-eee," he howled, over and over.

That first day was a nightmare. We hit snag after hang-up, and whoever the real estate company hired to fall the logs, fell them up and down the hill instead of across, like they figured we was gonna Cat-log the place. The first crack out of the box, 'ol Hal took off on foot to find the fallers and see if he could straighten 'em out. We had to keep changing road, and couldn't get no production; the logs laying like they was.

Come quittin' time we was beat; we'd only got eight loads a' logs. The guy from the real estate company wasn't happy, and neither was Hal. "Better cut them trucks back," Hal told the guy, "till we get out a' this area."

The man walked away shakin' his head, got in his Lincoln Navigator and drove off. You could tell by lookin' at him, this wasn't his game. Him runnin' around in them flatlander hiking boots that cost a fortune and only showd a smidgen of leather, and sporting a brand new Filson timber cruising jacket too.

Stubby called him a scissorbill.

We all ate at the diner that night, then went down the street to the motel to sack out. All the time we were eating Harley kept pumping one of the evening waitresses about the girl who waited on him that morning. But if she knew anything, she wasn't tellin' Harley. She was kind of a homely girl herself, friendly, but tall and boney with thick glasses.

I slept like a rock that night, and when I got up I was sore all over. My fingers was really sore—a sign I hadn't set chokers in a while.

The waitress with the good butt was back at work the following morning, and Harley was hot after her, teasing her about her job, telling her he could get her on setting chokers up at the yarder. "It'd pay a lot more than this," Harley told her, with a wink, "and just think of the fringe benefits."

But she wasn't one to sit there and take it—she gave as good as she got. "You don't know how much I make," she told him. "I probably make more in tips from guys like you than a choker setter makes all day."

Even Hal had to laugh at that one.

When we got ready to leave, Harley tried to pull her out the door with him, but she slapped his hands and told him, "You're gonna be late for work."

Again, all the way to the landing, all Harley could talk about was "the ass on that waitress."

Later, just after changing road, and half an hour before lunch, he came over, sat down beside us as a turn a' logs was going in, and said, "I don't even know her name."

That afternoon Harley was in rare form, dancing on the logs after they been whistled to the landing—just before the riggin' got tight and the floor of the forest started to move all over. He kept laughing and telling jokes. He even told the one about the Indian boy named Two Dogs Fucking; he told it to Paul, who'd never heard it before.

He'd hoot out the yarder signals, like an owl, seconds before I could send 'em in on the Talky-Tooter, and he'd stand on the end of the last log to do a jig in his calk boots just as the turn started for the landing.

These were dangerous antics, but Harley was in love and the rest of us thought it was all hilarious.

On Friday, Harley was late to breakfast, and the waitress with the good butt was late too. Stubby winked at Hal, who just shook his head with a knowing smile and turned back to his coffee.

Harley was into his howls, laughs, and gestures again that morning. He even did that dancing-in-place thing, like them Russian Cossacks do in the movies, with his arms crossed in front of him, one foot out and then the other. He did it on a huge sugar pine stump with his calk boots kicking up little splinters of wood.

But the first thing after lunch, a turn of logs tore loose a monstrous red cedar stump up on the hill above us. When it came rolling back down the hill, Harley found himself in a bad spot. He managed to dive in behind a small rock outcropping just in time, and the giant stump bounced over his head before crashing down the hill toward the river.

"Whoo-eee," Harley howled, "I could see the ants crawlin' around on that sum-bitch."

The close call with the big stump calmed Harley down a little. Then the last truck of the day called in with a flat tire, so we knocked off half an hour early.

Most of the crew decided to take the crummy back to Yoncalla for the weekend, but Hal had to stay to keep the fallers lined out. Plus, the old Cat skinner on the Eight needed another piece of road flagged out.

Harley decided to stay too, and we all knew why, but nobody said nothing.

I hadn't been home for more than an hour when Harley's wife called, wantin' to know why he didn't come back with the rest of us. I told her he had to stay and help Hal, trying to keep my voice calm as I said it. I never told anyone what was really going on, not my ex-wife, not my girlfriend, not even my old man when I went over to split up some firewood for him on Sunday.

We left again late Sunday afternoon and got to the job about nine o'clock that night. There was no sign of Harley, so we went over to Hal's room to check in with him.

But Harley was at the diner the next morning for breakfast, and while the waitress with the good butt waited on him, the two of them didn't say one word to each other. They didn't even make eye contact.

We was all dying to find out what had gone on over the weekend, so when we piled into the crummy, we were kinda surprised when Harley kept his silence.

He couldn't hold it for long, though. We all knew he wouldn't, and about half way to the job he began to open up. "That little girl is a real live wire," he started in. "Whoo-eee."

He told us about how the first night he had to talk real hard to get her to come to his room. "And then the next night, she just come on over," he said, "like she'd always lived there."

Once we started yardin' logs Harley began with his horsing around—playing tricks on the choker setters, doing little jigs on the logs.

That night, when we got back to the motel, Harley went straight to his room, and the next morning, while Paul and I was standing outside, waiting for the rest of the crew, Good Butt came scurrying out a' Harley's room, jumped in a little white car, and left.

"It's a good thing Stubby wasn't here to see that," Paul said. "We'd a' never heard the end of it."

Forty-five minutes later, at the diner, Harley and the waitress went through their routine of not speaking to each other. She even waited on me and Paul this time. She got the older woman to serve Rich and Harley.

We didn't climb up to the landing to eat lunch that day. It was just too steep. We were loggin' out a deep corner clear out at the end of the mainline, and we had to keep changing road without getting anywhere near the top of the hill. And while we were sitting there, talking about this or that, Harley blurted out, "She's got an old man."

Of course there wasn't any doubt about who he was talking about, so we just sat there and waited for more.

Finally, he went on with, "He was a sliver-picker—pulled green chain at a mill around here someplace. Got laid off a few years back when the mill went down and got into meth. Now he don't do nothin' but tweak and cook meth. She says he's got a lab set up somewhere down river."

A few minutes after that, Stubby slithered the riggin' back down the hill, and we went back to work.

Along about two thirty in the afternoon something went haywire with the yarder. We got word through the talky-tooter we were gonna be down for about twenty minutes, so we all sat down to take a breather.

Harley went on with what he was saying "She says he's just a ghost of his former self—her old man—and he goes for three or four days without sleeping. Sometimes he gets mean, real mean His teeth have turned black and he's starting to lose 'em. Don't seem to care.

"She says he's got so skinny and feeble, she thinks she could take 'im in a fair fight. 'Course, he don't fight fair. She's afraid to live with 'im, and afraid to leave 'im. Scared of what he might do."

We all sat there in silence for a moment. Then I asked, without looking at Harley directly, "So she has to go home every night to that?"

I could feel Harley's eyes on me, but I didn't turn in his direction. "Her old man stays down at the meth lab most of the time," he said. "Only comes home when he needs somethin', which ain't often."

We went back to work after that, and finished the day in relative silence.

But the next morning Harley was in rare form. Paul and I got up in time to see the waitress leave his room. Then her and Harley went through their silent routine again at breakfast, but as soon as he jumped out of the crummy onto the landing he started singin' "O Sole Mio," pretending to be singing in Italian, with his arms flung out wide, waving his hands like a goalie.

'Course, we knew he wasn't no Italian, but none of us knew the language, so he could a' been using anything for words. We wouldn't know the difference. "Ain't he a character," Paul said to me, as Harley started running out of plausible vowel-ending syllables, and switched over to Elvis's, "It's

Now or Never."

And I had to agree. If Harley was anything at all, he was a character. But it was later that afternoon when everything went wrong.

It was about an hour after lunch, and hot and dry enough that we were afraid a' being shut down for hoot-owl. We'd just set the chokers on a turn of medium-sized red fir logs, and was beginning to run out a' the turn, when Harley decided to dance on the end of the logs as they started to move.

It was a double risky move. He wasn't only playing with fire by staying too close to the logs, but he was in the bight of the haul-back to boot. Meaning if the tail hold pulled loose, the haul-back—a 7/8 inch steel cable stretched tighter 'n a fiddle string—would sizzle back through the unit and cut him in half on its way through.

I started to reach for my talky-tooter to cut off the turn. I knew it would make Harley mad, but this was ridiculous. But just as I started to grab the damn thing, Harley barked.

I looked up to see a black cloud billow up from under the logs. It took a moment to recognize it as a mad swarm of bald-faced hornets. I stood there tryin' to figure out what to do. I could see they'd built a nest in a tan oak, but a big fir tree had been felled across it, pushing the tan oak down without breaking it. The hornets' nest had been forced down close to the ground, but it stayed in one piece, so the hornets continued to use it.

'Course, when we started dragging logs across it, them black and white bastards was hell-bent to get even with whoever was responsible.

Harley'd barked when the first hornet stung him, and he slapped the back of his neck. The other choker setters were running up the hill, tryin' to get away from the hornets, but I had the second talky-tooter. I had to cut off the turn. Harley had the other one, but was beyond thinking about using it.

The problem was, just as I reached for the talky-tooter, a choker smacked a tanoak and hurled a short piece of limb about two feet off the ground, like a boomerang, that hit the tooter right below the trigger. The batteries fell out of the thing, and then I began to get stung.

I'm here to tell ya, them bald hornet stings hurt like nothing I ever felt before, but I had to get that damn tooter back together, and get a signal off to the landing. I could see Paul, up the hill, waving his tin hat in the air, trying to get the attention of somebody on the landing. But I couldn't even see

Harley, through the black cloud of hornets.

Then I could feel my hands and eyes swelling up from the stings I'd taken. I couldn't get my fingers to bend enough to pick the batteries up off the ground.

When the riggin' came tight again, the hornets thinned a little. One of the chokers was looped around Harley's outstretched arm. When the chokers snapped shut and the slack snapped out of the mainline, a violent wire-rope-tug jerked the arm from Harley's body.

With the limbs snapping the haul-back flopping and the roar of the yarder up on the hill, I was the only one close enough to hear his scream.

Hornets continued to sting Harley's body, but a few stayed with the arm and went on to the landing with the logs.

I heard whoops and hollers from the landing. The fellas up there was just now getting stung. Then I heard the kid chasin' landing yell, "JE-SUS FUCKIN' CHRIST." He yelled it like somebody'd just drove a stake through his heart. Of course, that meant he'd found the arm.

There was nothing I could do for Harley. He couldn't have lasted more that a few seconds after the yarder jerked his arm off, so I started for the landing. The problem was, my eyes was almost swelled shut. I couldn't see nothing and my diaphragm muscles didn't seem to work. I couldn't get no air.

After a few minutes I could hear Hal and Stubby. I couldn't see a thing, but one of 'em had a hand under my armpit. Then there was a hand under my other armpit and they started dragging me up the hill.

The next thing I heard was sirens.

When I woke up it was night out and I was in a hospital room. The overhead light was on and the television set was tuned to one a' them dumb sitcoms. It felt like my whole body was vibrating and my teeth hurt.

I looked over to see Paul laying in the bed next to me. The first words out of his mouth were, "You ought 'a see the nurse."

She came in a few moments later—a woman in her sixties who must have weighed four hundred pounds—and she was full of cutsie-nursey phrases, like, "How are we tonight?" and, "You gave us quite a fright."

She wrote something down on the clipboards at the ends of our beds, and left. Once she was out of earshot, Paul said, "Feel like you been up for three weeks drinkin' strong coffee?"

"Yeah," I said, feeling my body vibrate. "I do feel that way."

"It's the adrenalin," he said. "They gave us both a great big slug of the stuff. It's supposed to get you breathing again.

"I was still awake when we got here. You was almost a goner. We're in Yreka."

It turned out Paul tried to get back down the hill to help me, but he'd been overwhelmed by the hornets, so Rich and the landing chaser had to come back down after him. The folks at the hospital kept a couple of the other fellas for a few hours of observation, but Paul and I were the only ones had to stay overnight.

The doctor came in a little later—young man, dark-rimmed glasses, kind of a nervous fella—and he told me I was lucky to be alive.

'Course, after he left I got to thinking about what had happened, and I didn't really feel all that lucky.

The sheriff's department and OSHA were both investigating the accident. We'd be down for a while, probably a week or more. So we moved out of our motel rooms. But just as we were leaving the scissorbill from the real estate company came by to talk to Hal.

He had a big glob 'a white shit on the end of his nose, which was way big enough to start with. It made him look like a circus clown—an angry circus clown. I had to turn away so he couldn't see me laughing

Once we were loaded up in the crummy and headed back to Yoncalla, I asked Paul, "What the hell was that white shit on the end of that dizzy idiot's nose?"

Paul laughed. "He showed up on the landing that day, just after the first ambulance got there. Minute he got out of his Navigator, and started to open his mouth, one a' them hornets nailed 'im on the end of the nose. Shut 'im right up," Paul continued. "He jumped in his Navigator and left."

We all moped around town for the next several days. Drank a lot a' beer, but we didn't see much of each other. Harley's funeral was the following Monday. We were all there for that.

It kinda made me a little mad. The preacher guy who was talking over Harley's casket obviously didn't know nothing about Harley. He never said one word about how Harley could dance like a Russian Cossack on a sugar pine stump with calk shoes—or how he could sing "O Sole Mio," and go on for ten minutes without knowing one word of Italian. The fella just rambled on about how Harley had been a boy scout once, and talked about some athletic awards he'd won in high school.

When it was all over, I walked away feeling like we'd buried the wrong guy.

It was a whole 'nother week before they cleared us to go back to work. The investigation didn't find where nobody'd done nothing wrong. They blamed the whole thing on the hornets.

"Harley was in love," Paul howled, on our way back down south that Sunday night, "that's what caused it."

And he was probably right, but after thinking about it, I couldn't come up with no good way one a' them investigators could a' got love to fit very well into an OSHA report, so the hornets were probably the next best option.

The company sent a new guy down to help set chokers, and they made me the riggin' slinger. Paul took over my job as lead choker setter. We'd both make a little more money, but it didn't seem to mean much, under the circumstances.

That first morning when I got up and realized I was supposed to drive the crummy, I felt kinda funny. I really didn't like myself very much for it, somehow.

Nobody said much of anything when we went back to work. The whole crew just moped around like they didn't care to be there.

Our production went way down. I just couldn't get the crew fired up the way Harley used to do, and when we went up to the landing on Wednesday to eat lunch, that real estate guy was there yelling at Hal.

I heard Hal ask the guy, "You want us to get somebody else killed?"

I tried to get around to see if the guy still had a blob a' white shit on the end of his nose, but he turned real quick and stomped back over to his car.

I pulled Hal aside and told him how I was sorry we weren't getting more logs. "I'm just afraid to take the chances Harley used to take," I told him.

"I don't want you taking them kind a' chances," Hal said. "You're doin' a good job."

The rest of the crew started picking on the new guy, like somehow it was his fault Harley wasn't with us anymore. I kept trying to intervene, but there's only so much a fella can do. And the drive back to Yoncalla on the weekends was pretty much a silent affair both going and coming.

The waitress with the good butt came to my room the second night after we got back. She was kinda drunk and she was toting one a' them four-packs of wine coolers. She was going on about Harley, and how she could have made him happy, and how awful she felt about everything and …

I didn't know how serious Harley was about the girl, but she thought he was serious, and that's all that mattered now.

I sat down and had a wine cooler with her, and what happened after that I don't really want to talk about. But when I got up to go to work the next morning, she was sleeping so sound you couldn't a' woke 'er with a cannon.

I was hoping none of the crew would see her little white car in the parking lot, and they didn't. I didn't either.

When we got back that night, she was gone and we never saw her again. She never came back to work at the diner and we never saw her around the motel. A couple days later, the local weekly newspaper came out with a front page story about the sheriff's office busting a local meth lab. When Paul and I read it, we were able to piece together from what Harley'd told us that the meth cooker was Good Butt's old man.

"Looks twenty years older than her," Paul observed.

"Probably the meth," I told him.

The meth bust took place on the same night she came to my motel room, which told me three things: she must have turned him in, she knew not to go home that night, and she needed a place to stay. I wasn't sure how I felt about all of that, but I didn't wish the girl no ill will.

In fact, that following Saturday evening, after having a few beers in my living room, I felt compelled to stand up and offer a toast in the mirror. "Here's to you, Good Butt," I said, in a loud boisterous voice. "May you find what you're lookin' for and always be happy."

My girlfriend was there at the time, and asked, "What in the world are you doing?"

"It was something I had to do for a friend," I told her.

She kept looking at me kinda weird all through the rest of the weekend.

Nothing much changed on the loggin' side, though. The crew continued to mope around and the drives back and forth to the job remained lifeless and silent.

But then, on the following Thursday morning, the older waitress let out a noise like a chicken when Stubby, the short, stocky yarder puncher, reached out and pinched her on the ass as she went by the counter with a load of dirty dishes.

Rousseau's War

Colette Tennant

I will not ask why death
rides a carousel horse, nor why death
raises the sickle-shaped banner,
nor why death brandishes a sabered claw,
nor about death. I will not ask why
death is a young girl in white –
in a dress, though ragged, still purer than
the whitest corpse at her feet.

Meet the Contributors

Colette Tennant is an English Professor at Corban University in Salem, Oregon where she teaches creative writing and literature courses. Her poetry book, Commotion of Wings, was published in 2010. Her poems have also been included in Southern Poetry Review, Cloudbank, Dos Passos Review and others.

Mary Arana is a fourth-grade teacher in Salem, Oregon. She graduated from George Fox University with a Bachelor of Arts in Writing/Literature and a Master of Arts in Teaching. Each day she leaves the classroom with pockets full of intercepted notes and gratitude for the opportunity to learn with a roomful of nine-year-olds. Her favorite way spend a weekend is going on a hike or run with her husband and baby daughter.

Marc Janssen is a veteran of the Ventra poetry scene. In the past 20 years he has been published in a variety of places both on-line and in journals and magazines. A graduate of California Lutheran University, he is currently employed by the state of Oregon. www.facebook/marcjanssenpoet.

Dan Encarnacion, a native of the San Francisco Bay Area, lives in Portland, Oregon. The bleak of Bela Tarr, the spare of Supersilent, and the spike of quad-lattes will stimulate his mind. He has received an MFA in Writing from the California College of the Arts. Dan has recently been published in *Fault Lines Poetry* (for which he also designed the cover) and *The Berkeley Poetry Review*; and online by *Eleven Eleven* and *The Red River Review*. In 2012, Dan will be published in *The Magic Lantern Review* and *Upstairs at Duroc*.

Rick Stoddart often writes poetry during meetings. He is a librarian and scholar at Oregon State University. He has lived in many states including this one.

Tim Pfau is a husband, father, grandfather who travels, reads, and writes full time. He serves on the Board of the Oregon Poetry Association. www.oregonpoets.org If sharing isn't the goal, why write it down?

Thomas Logan has a variety of literary and pulp stories appearing in online and print publications and has worked in various capacities for Fictional International and smaller journals. Most recently, he's served as Fiction Editor for Issue 6 of the Portland, Ore. literary journal The Grove Review. Semi-reclusive and secretive, he'd prefer you not to know that he got his MFA in 2006, has lived and taught across the country, or that he often ends his sentences awkwardly.

Allyson Myers is going into her junior year at Willamette University majoring in English, with a concentration in creative writing. She usually writes fiction (both short stories and novels, though I have yet to finish one...) but she recently started getting into poetry writing and enjoying the process of learning this markedly different form of expression. Outside of writing she enjoys playing soccer, travelling (she loves airports) and playing with her cat Garfield.

John Byrne lives in Albany, Oregon with his wife, Cheryl French, an artist, and their high school age daughter. He writes short poems, short stories, and short plays. One of his poems is in the first edition of the Gold Man Review. Others have appeared in The Lyric, 14 by 14, Lucid Rhythms, Umbrella Journal and other print and internet journals as well as in two anthologies, Many Trails to the Summit (Rose Alley Press, Seattle, 2010) and Love Notes (Vagabondage Press, Florida, 2012). His plays have been staged in New York City, Fremont, Ca., Independence, Missouri, Seattle, Albany and Corvallis.

Chelsea Bieker was raised in California's Central Valley. She has an MFA in Creative Writing from Portland State University, where she teaches undergraduate writing classes. Her work recently won a finalist award in Glimmer Train's March Fiction Open, and is forthcoming in The Normal School Literary Magazine. She is at work on a collection of stories. She hopes to one day own a wolf.

Robert Bennet used to work in the woods as a logger, but when Ronald Reagan got elected it marked the end of everything positive in Oregon. After relocating to California, with an idea of survival, Robert wrote a 400 page fictional account for the purpose of getting even with Ronald Reagan. Nobody was much interested in publishing the book, so he went to Sacramento State and earned an MA in Creative Writing.

By the time he completed the degree, Reagan's handlers had come clean with the public, admitted he suffered from Alzheimer's, and had his teleprompter unplugged . So he wrote some other novels. He continue to write short stories and submit them to literary publications.

Patrick Hannon will be receiving an MFA in Creative Writing at Portland State University this December.

Amy Miller's poems have appeared recently in Northwest Review, Willow Springs, Many Mountains Moving, ZYZZYVA, and the anthology What the River Brings: Oregon River Poems. A finalist for the 49th Parallel Award and the Pablo Neruda Prize, she won the Cultural Center of Cape Cod National Poetry Competition, judged by Tony Hoagland. She lives in Ashland, Oregon.

Mike Ritchey is a retired newspaper owner and publisher from the San Juan Mountains in western Colorado, soon to enter his second year in the MFA Creative Writing-Fiction program at Portland State University. He is currently working on a novel, and "Mary Lou's Make-Over" is his first published story.

Michael Snider resides in Grants Pass where he has lived and worked most of his life. Michael retired at the end of 2010 after working twenty-five years for Josephine County as a land use planner. The last ten years he served as the county's planing director. Before that he worked eleven years as an attorney, arbitrator and mediator. Michael is a happy retiree, serving on the boards of several non-profits, writing fiction and non-fiction, and photographing landscapes and grandchildren.

Grahame Watt is a rising junior at Reed College who hails from the same Chicago suburb that birthed such greats as Ernest Hemingway, Ray Kroc, and Homer Simpson. A Political Science major interested in international relations, he consistently feels guilty whenever he skims over articles about Syria and the Eurozone in favor of the crossword page. He turns 21 this October, but he'll be abroad, so really it's no big deal.

Nyla Alisia is both an award-winning poet and photographer. Her works can be found in numerous publications and websites worldwide. Nyla is the founder and host of three international poetry radio shows, The SpeakEasy Cafe, The Inkwell, and Re-verse. She also teaches creative vision photography and writing workshops.

Lois Rosen is a retired Chemeketa Community College ESL teacher who teaches writing at Willamette University. Traprock Books published her poetry book, *Pigeons*. Her stories and poems have appeared in numerous magazines including: *Willow Springs, Calyx, and Northwest Review*. She enjoys living in Salem with her husband and her cat, Pauline.

CPSIA information can be obtained at www.ICGtesting.com
Printed in the USA
BVOW081123181112

305848BV00001B/81/P